Tech Mod Mania with Yoshi

A Guide to Customizing Your Computer and Other Digital Devices

Joshua "Yoshi" DeHerrera

Contents at a Glance

To my father, Alan DeHerrera.
You taught me many important lessons. You helped me to not be afraid, to put everything on the line. Without your constant support and nurturing of my creative and sometimes destructive tinkering I would not be who I am today. You made this all possible.

TechTV's Mod Mania with Yoshi:
A Guide to Customizing Your Computer and Other Digital Devices

Copyright © 2004 by Pearson Education

Published by TechTV Press, in association with Peachpit Press, a division of Pearson Education.

Peachpit Press
800 E. 96th Street, 3rd Floor, Indianapolis, Indiana 46240

International Standard Book Number: 0-7357-1405-3

Library of Congress Catalog Card Number: 2003109153

Printed in the United States of America

First printing: November, 2003

08 07 06 05 04 03   7 6 5 4 3 2 1

Interpretation of the printing code: The rightmost double-digit number is the year of the book's printing; the rightmost single-digit number is the number of the book's printing. For example, the printing code 03-1 shows that the first printing of the book occurred in 2003.

Trademarks

All terms mentioned in this book that are known to be trademarks or service marks have been appropriately capitalized. Pearson Education cannot attest to the accuracy of this information. Use of a term in this book should not be regarded as affecting the validity of any trademark or service mark.

Warning and Disclaimer

Every effort has been made to make this book as complete and as accurate as possible, but no warranty of fitness is implied. The information is provided on an as-is basis. The authors and the publisher shall have neither liability nor responsibility to any person or entity with respect to any loss or damages arising from the information contained in this book.

Bulk Purchases/Corporate Sales

The publisher offers discounts on this book when ordered in quantity for bulk purchases and special sales. For sales within the U.S., please contact: Corporate and Government Sales at (800)382-3419 or corpsales@pearsontechgroup.com. Outside of the U.S., please contact: International Sales at (317)581-3793 or international@pearsontechgroup.com.

Publisher
Nancy Ruenzel

Associate Publisher
Stephanie Wall

TechTV, Vice President, Strategic Development
Glenn Farrell

Production Manager
Gina Kanouse

TechTV Press Project Manager
Sasha Zullo

Acquisitions Editor
Wendy Sharp

Development/Copy Editor
Anne Marie Walker

Project Editor/Compositor
Michael Thurston

Senior Indexer
Cheryl Lenser

Proofreader
Debbie Williams

Manufacturing Coordinator
Dan Uhrig

Cover and Interior Designer
Alan Clements

Cover Photo
David S. Rubin

Marketing
Scott Cowlin
Tammy Detrich
Hannah Onstad Latham

Publicity Manager
Susan Nixon

650 Townsend Street
San Francisco, California 94103

Table of Contents

About the Author

Joshua "Yoshi" DeHerrera is Segment Producer/Technical Specialist for *The Screen Savers* on TechTV. He also runs one of the most popular hardware modding destinations on the web at www.yoshi.us. He attended the California Polytechnic State University in San Luis Obispo and loves anything to do with computers, cars, motorcycles, and of course, modding them all.

About the Technical Reviewer

This reviewer contributed his considerable hands-on expertise to the entire development process for **TechTV's Mod Mania with Yoshi: A Guide to Customizing Your Computer and Other Digital Devices**. As the book was being written, this dedicated professional reviewed all the material for technical content, organization, and flow. His feedback was critical to ensuring that this book fits our readers' needs for the highest-quality technical information.

Lee Holburn is the resident graphics artist for www.moddin.net, one of the most popular computer modification sites on the web. In addition, he regularly reviews and modifies computer equipment for the web site and can be considered a "Jack of all trades" when it comes to computers. He attended Napier University based in Edinburgh, Scotland and loves anything to do with computers, art, and technology.

Acknowledgments

A very special thanks goes to the contributing modders: Chris Adams, Jerami Campbell, Paul Capello, Barry Collins, Joe Klingler, Jeff Neima, Gareth Powell, Jeffrey L. Stephenson, Mikko Syrjälä, and Rainer Wingende. They have shared their wonderful creations and hard work with us. They serve as an inspiration to me and hopefully to you all.

As I have said before, I am very lucky to have the honor of knowing many very talented and unique people. Along the way, all of you have proved invaluable in my adventures and projects.

My friends (and family) Tuy, Michael, Robbo, Colin, Katherine, and all the rest of the crew, well…where do I start? You are part of the adventures that have shaped me. You have all contributed to my projects, to my very life. Your input and ideas are invaluable to me. Most of all, you have all put up with my mods not only taking over my apartment but at times yours as well. Just remember I got your back.

To the TechTV and *The Screen Savers* staff—wow this is a big list—I have to thank every single member. Working at TechTV has been one of the best experiences I have had. This is one of the most talented groups I have had the honor to work with. Your support has been crucial. Thank you Leo, Pat, Paul, Gregg, Peter, Ken, Roman, Kevin, Dan, Joshua, David, Kim, Sarah, Morgan, Nicole (both of you), Josh, Porter, and everyone else. I can't begin to say how much each of you has helped me out—by listening to my rants, weird ideas, and simply by helping me make it all happen.

To Sasha, Wendy, Megan, Anne Marie, and Glenn, you have helped me take an idea and make it into this book. I would not have had a clue how to do this without your help and guidance.

Chapter 1

What Is Modding?

It is very difficult to make a blanket statement about modding. One of the great things about modding is that it has a unique meaning to each of us. Like any other form of art, modding is an expression of who you are. That said, modding is the art of customizing your computer or other machines, changing them so that they look better, perform better, and *are* better.

For me, the core of modding is about expressing myself. It is a look inside my personality. It is about creation, about discovery. This discovery often makes me feel like a little kid learning something new: It may be a big thing or a small thing, but learning it is a triumph. That is why I have so much fun with it.

How Did I Get into Modding?

I honestly don't remember how I got into modding. Since I was a little kid I have been taking almost everything apart around the house. And of course, I ruined my share of gadgets that were not supposed to be messed with.

The first big project that stands out in my mind was my motorcycle. I started by changing the exhaust to add a little power and give it a nice raspy sound. Then I had to upgrade the suspension, brakes, bodywork, cooling system, engine, fuel system, and so on. Do you see a pattern here? Modding starts out small, but unavoidably, it becomes its own entity. Like any living entity, you grow to love these projects because there is so much of yourself in them.

Thinking back, I had saved for so long just to get my beast, but once I had it, it just didn't feel as if it were mine. Painting it seemed like a good idea. After all, painting would identify it as mine because nobody else would have the exact same paint job. Once it looked good, I needed more power—more power is always better, right? But that road was a long and twisting one. Many components tie in to affect performance, so it's not as simple as a single upgrade. Once everything else was fabricated, tested, and final, I took it all apart and painted it again—the right way. This time each layer was hand sanded, hand rubbed, and given many layers of wax. This baby was a beauty. But I'm not talking about a motorcycle; I'm talking about my computer.

The art of modding is based on these principles: better, stronger, faster, and most importantly, unique.

What Drives Modders?

The basic modding principles only touch the tip of the iceberg, however. There are so many facets to modding. You might start out by simply taking things apart and trying to understand what makes them work. But from there it grows exponentially.

Part of the fun is the process of discovery. Only by learning and expanding our minds do we really truly live. I'm not afraid to try new things. Just because nobody has ever done it doesn't mean it is not possible. Of course, it also doesn't mean it is. But I like to find these things out for myself. The process is like a puzzle that I eagerly dive into.

And then there's the challenge. There is something very satisfying about encountering a problem, solving it, and then preparing for the next problem. It is very empowering and is probably the main reason I really enjoy modding.

Of course, I like the competition, too. I think a lot of modders are fueled by the desire to impress their friends. They like making unique machines, something people will "ooh" and "aah" over. In this sense, competition drives modders to do more and more creative things. But I'm also motivated by the desire to impress myself: I want to build something that will make me say, "Wow! I actually made that."

How To Use This Book

As someone interested in modding, you probably want the satisfaction of the "Wow" factor as well; after all, you've picked up this book! Whether you're completely new to modding or have tried a few mods of your own, this book can provide you with ideas, suggestions, tips, and plenty of fun challenges to get you started.

In the second section of the book, you'll see some of the mods that I've done over the years, including some that you may have seen previously on *The Screen Savers*. Creating cool mods for the show is one of the best parts of my job, and in this section of the book, you'll see those mods, plus get some step-by-step instructions and tips for how you can replicate them or do similar mods of your own.

From custom-painting, creating windows, and adding lights, to some of my most extreme mods—such as creating a computer from an ammo box (Project YM-23) or including all my game machines in a single box (Project Y-Boxx)—this section of the book will teach you what you need to know to complete your own great mods.

But the key to modding is originality and creativity, and that you can't learn from a book. Or can you? In the third section of the book, "Yoshi's Favorites," you'll get inspiration from seeing and reading about more than a dozen of my favorite mods from around the world. Some of these mods are just simply cool. Others are built so well that the talent and drive needed to create such nice mods is inspiring in itself. These mods are just a small sample of what exists. There are many, many more mods that we just don't have the space to include. To find more, explore the web, and use mods you like as inspiration for your own endeavors in modding.

I hope you enjoy the pages in this book. Although it is only a small taste of the modding scene, it is also a glimpse inside the mind of the modder. Next time you meet someone who has tricked out their case, you will know what they really did, and how much work they put into it. And if you need some advice or just want to check out the scene, head on over to my forums at `http://yoshi.us/forums`, where you will find a community that helps each other and gladly shares its ideas. While you're there, post a picture of your mod, I would love to see it!

Joshua "Yoshi" DeHerrera
The Mad Modder
TechTV, *The Screen Savers*

Chapter 2

Setting Up a Home Workshop

Whether you are a modder, a gear head, an artist, or a do-it-yourselfer, having a home workshop appeals to a lot of us. Most people think you have to have tons of free space to have a home workshop. However, I have found that you can have a useable workspace in almost any amount of space if you plan it carefully.

A workshop usually consists of three main elements: a workbench, tools, and supplies. If you keep a few things in mind when setting up your workshop, you should be able to assemble a versatile work space in which to complete your projects:

- Maximize your space
- Apply ergonomics
- Use proper tools
- Ensure cleanliness and order

> **This chapter does not describe the proper techniques of using each type of tool. Suffice it to say that if you do not know how to use a tool safely, ask someone that does to show you. And always, *always* use proper eye and ear protection.**

The Workbench

Whatever type of workspace you are using, there are a few details you need to consider:

- **Table surface.** Hard rubber has many advantages. The most important advantage for modding purposes is that hard rubber is nonconductive and is safe for delicate materials. It also holds up to lots of hammering and pounding. If you don't have space for a stationary, rubber-top table, try to purchase a medium thickness rubber mat for your tabletop.

- **Lighting.** For good visibility when working and to preserve your eyesight, lighting is a very important factor. Halogen lights are a nice option for maximum brightness. Not only will you want your area to be as bright as possible, but you will also want a variety of lamps that can be moved around and adjusted to different working heights and conditions.

- **Magnifying lens.** Office supply stores as well as electronic supply stores carry an assortment of magnifying lenses. The nicer lenses can be very expensive but are not necessary for modding purposes. Prices can range from $50–$600; the difference between lenses is the level of magnification, size of the lens, and lighting. I recommend purchasing one with lighting because it makes soldering small components a piece of cake.

- **Chair.** A good chair will keep you comfortable and in turn make it easier for you to work. Don't skimp on purchasing a quality chair.

- **Storage.** Organization, especially in a small space, is a must. Storage areas can be built into your workbench, modular wall brackets can be utilized, or closeable plastic bins can hold your tools and supplies. You'll want a lot of storage, so be creative and use whatever you need to keep your area neat and orderly.

Tools

The types of tools in your workshop can vary from a simple collection to a vast array depending on your uses, the space you have available, and how long you have been collecting them. When you buy a tool, try to buy the best quality tool. High-quality tools can last a lifetime if you take good care of them. When gathering a collection of tools, start with the most common ones and slowly add to your collection over time. If you go out and buy every tool you think you need, you will find that you need tools you don't have and have tools you don't need. Start with a good, basic set of tools and purchase others as you need them.

Basic Tools

Most people have a few basic tools for minor repairs around the house. But if you don't, here are a few suggestions to start your collection:

- **Screwdrivers.** Try to get a good standard set of each type of screwdriver: Phillips, flat head, Torx, and hex head. (Try to get ball hex drivers if possible.) The most useful screwdrivers will be the smaller sizes. A jeweler's set and a couple of long blade screwdrivers in Phillips and flat head will come in very handy as well.

- **Nut drivers.** Be sure to get a basic set in both standard and metric versions. I prefer to use a 1/4" socket set so I can use the ratchet handle if I need extra leverage.

- **Soldering iron.** A good variable temperature model is best because you will need to use lower temperatures with more delicate circuits. Get a variety of tip sizes as well.

- **Diagonal cutters.** For all kinds of cutting jobs, you'll need diagonal cutters with different heads: straight, angled, and curved. Make sure you have a large heavy-duty pair of straight cutters as well because thicker metals will ruin the small cutters.

- **Magnetizer/demagnetizer.** A great tool for reaching those small parts that fall into tight places.

- **Pliers.** A basic collection of pliers is a must. You will want standard heavy-duty pliers, needle-nose pliers, wire strippers, a crimper, and some vise grips.

- **Files.** A good selection of needle files and large machinist files will be very helpful.

- **Knives/cutting tools.** A utility knife and X-acto knives with small and large handles as well as a variety of blades will make cutting easier. A hacksaw and a jeweler's saw are also very useful items.

- **Dremel tool (or clone).** A rotary tool with a good selection of bits, burs, and cutters is used a lot.

- **Cutting mat.** A good cutting mat will keep your table in tip-top shape. Most art supply stores sell self-healing cutting mats.

- **Digital multimeter.** A decent multimeter with small probes, micro probes, and alligator clips will prove indispensable.

- **Cordless drill.** I prefer a cordless drill because it is not only useful in a workshop, but also can be used around the house.

Advanced Tools

As you become more experienced with power tools, you will want to add to your tool collection. Here are a few advanced tools you might not be able to live without:

- **Drill press.** One of the most useful items to have in a workshop. Whether you are making a small circuit board or a large panel, a drill press allows you to be far more accurate than you would be with a hand drill. You might also want to invest in a vise for the drill press with v-blocks for round stock.

- **Band saw.** One of those tools that makes you say to yourself, "Why did I never have one of these before?" A small tabletop model is all most people need. A band saw allows for very precise cuts to be made in wood, plastic, and thin-gauge, soft metals. With the change of a blade, it can also cut ferrous metals. But a high-powered model is better for cutting steel.

- **Vises.** A large anvil-type vise; a multi-axis, adjustable, soft-jaw vise; and helping hands are tools you will use for everything from model making and electronics to fixing things around the house.

- **Torches.** A butane pen torch is useful for small precise heating, and a large propane torch is essential for heavy-duty usage. As with all tools, remember to keep safety in mind, especially when using a torch of any kind.

- **Optional tools.** A table saw, cable tester, jigsaw, rotary sander, and a variable output power supply round out the more advanced tools.

Supplies

The supplies you will need are many, and they tend to become greater in number as you work through a project. Usually, you will have to buy a lot more supplies than you need for any particular project.

Here are some you can start with:

- **Glues.** Various glues are used all the time for projects as well as for minor household repairs. Make sure you have a good supply of super glue (cyanocrylate), epoxy (both quick set and extended work time), and flexible adhesives such as silicon.

- **Sandpaper.** Another universal supply, sandpaper comes in a variety of grits and grades. I recommend using wet/dry grade in the 220–2000 grit range. It has a variety of uses, from painting to lapping heat sinks.

- **Solder, flux, and heat-shrink tubing.** Essential staples that are used for all electronic projects.

- **Zip ties.** Various sizes of zip ties are another necessity in a workshop.

- **Additional supplies.** Multipurpose items include wire in various sizes, electrical tape, duct tape, screws (keep all the screws left over from new cases, other devices, and so on), waterproof markers, and grease pencils.

Organization

A well-organized workshop is the difference between a slick professional environment and a tattered, hazardous mess of a space. Many different options for organization are available depending on the type of space you have. Some of the most universal organization aids are plastic parts bins with moveable dividers and closing covers. They are portable and can easily be stacked neatly out of the way. I like to have five or six empty parts bins to hold parts from projects; they make it easier to keep track of which parts are from what project, especially when I have many projects going on at the same time.

If you have shelving handy or can mount brackets on your wall, modular open-top bins can be used to store your consumables. Common sense dictates that you keep your most frequently used tools and supplies close by and within easy reach. Those used less frequently should be stored away.

Before you begin organizing your workspace, sit in your chair and clear your work-bench, desk, or table. Then imagine you are working. What tools will you need most often? What consumable supplies need constant access? Now organize your tools according to how often they are used. Try to keep the center of the table (the full width) open to use as your primary workspace.

If you can hang shelving or brackets, use the area directly in front of you so you can leave your tabletop free. Because the topside drawers in a desk are easily accessible, you can store your frequently used tools and supplies within reach. The key is to orga-nize your area so that you don't need to move your chair to reach the most commonly used items. More than likely, you will change the layout of your work space many times before you settle on one you really like; so don't make anything permanent (wall anchors, etc.) until you have tried it for a while first.

A good workshop is like a good story. It takes time to develop, but the best ones are never really finished. Building a nice workshop can be a matter of pride. When your friends come over looking for your help with a project, they will be impressed by how nice your workshop is. Take your time, do it properly, and your workshop will even make the pros jealous.

Chapter 3

Modding Your Case

A growing number of people are modifying their computer cases. And a growing number of people want to mod, but just don't have the time or resources. You're reading this book, so you're probably pretty interested in the idea; however, you might want to start out slowly.

Case Modding Without the Work: Products and Resources You Can Use for Instant Case Mods

Several manufacturers and boutique companies are now making and modifying cases for you. The prices can range from cheap to expensive, but I've found that you get what you pay for. The types of mods range from a standard case with a side window to cases with lighting, custom windows, custom window etchings, custom painting, and more.

Premodded Cases

The following list describes a variety of premodded cases available to you:

- **Enermax CS5190AL Red Aluminum Supertower.** On the high side as far as price goes, and its styling is something you either like or hate. Opinions have been split, but I like it.
- **Xoxide X-Viper.** The X-Viper is a budget-priced case that comes with a lot of options that usually only higher-priced units have. Its styling is nice, not too flashy but still trick.
- **Xoxide Clear Acrylic ATX Case.** Clear Plexiglas cases were something only the extreme modder would even think about building. Now you can buy one off the shelf.
- **Thermaltake Xaser III V2000A Super Tower.** The Xaser III is a very high-tech looking case. Its styling is modern. It comes with a 4-fan bay-bus control preinstalled, with temp monitoring function and overheat alarms. This is really nice for those that intend to overclock their system or just push it to its limits.

Get Mod Components

If you want to add components that require little or no handiwork, try shopping at the following retailers:

- Crazy PC (www.crazypc.com)
- PC Modifications (www.pcmods.com)
- Xoxide (www.xoxide.com)

These are good spots to find lights, fans, CPU coolers, or cases. Sometimes I browse the pages looking for new items that might give me ideas. Components can range from five to several hundred dollars depending on what you are interested in.

Custom Designs

The following companies offer custom-built or premodded complete systems:

- Falcon Northwest (www.falcon-nw.com)
- Xoxide (www.xoxide.com)
- DesignComp (www.designcomp.com)
- Alienware (www.alienware.com)

Alienware sells systems that are both custom-configured and painted in a color of your choice. This is a nice option because the tower, keyboard, mouse, and monitor are all painted to match each other.

Falcon Northwest can provide a system with custom-painted graphics, as shown in Figures 3.1 and 3.2. Check out the Exotix Gallery on its web site for ideas: Some of Falcon Northwest's designs are truly beautiful.

3.1 and 3.2 Stunning designs from Falcon Northwest.

TechTV's Mod Mania with Yoshi

Review: Alienware Area-51

Ultimate Gaming PC Gets a Makeover

By Robert Heron, TechTV Labs

Alienware's latest design will either leave you drooling or scratching your head in wonderment. See Figure 3.3.

3.3 Alienware's Area-51 system.

The company's latest über-gaming box retains the Area-51 name but sports a new look courtesy of a Giger-inspired case design. Twin air-intake grills on the front of the case wrap around the sides to form a pair of alien-looking eyes. Powering up the system reveals two glowing 80mm case fans behind the sculpted grills, completing the effect. With so many companies mimicking the Antec case style that Alienware previously used, the new design helps Alienware stand apart.

Externally, the "alien head" case offers four front-mounted USB 2.0 ports as well as a clever cable management rack attached to the rear of the system. We found the rounded rack quite functional and felt it gave the new Area-51 a finished look.

With a configured price of less than $2,600, our Area-51 was equipped with 1GB of 400 MHz DDR memory, a Pentium 4 3.0 GHz (800 MHz FSB) CPU, a 120GB 7200 RPM ATA hard drive, as well as an ATI Radeon 9800 Pro. Of course, Alienware also offers Microsoft's Internet Keyboard and IntelliMouse Explorer 3 custom-painted to match the case.

Alienware can configure a system to suit any taste. On our display options wish list was NEC's new LCD3000. This 30-inch, digital monster gives plasma a run for its money and will set you back a cool $4,200. If that isn't enough, a 40-inch model will be available soon.

The new Area-51 is a unique looking system built with premium parts that can be customized to your heart's (or wallet's) content. With performance equal to the best rigs available, Alienware's Area-51 has the muscle to back up its otherworldly appearance.

Specs: Pentium 4 3.0 GHz (800 MHz FSB); 1GB 400 MHz DDR; 120GB 7200 RPM ATA HD; ATI Radeon 9800 Pro (128MB); Sound Blaster Audigy 2 Platinum 6.1

Paint It

If you don't want to paint your computer yourself, consider contacting your local body shop painter, custom helmet painter, or motorcycle painter. Many of these artists are able to paint small components, and they do amazing work. You can usually choose almost any color of paint you can imagine. If you are interested in adding custom designs to your case, find an airbrush artist who can add cartoons, design logos, and more.

For additional information and ideas on modding, try going to the forums on modding and finding the extreme mods you like. Contact those members and see whether they would be willing to do the same modding for you.

Visit my forums at http://yoshi.us to check out what people are doing or to get help with your mods.

Project: Face-Lift

One of the simplest and most effective changes you can make is to paint the exterior of your case. Many people have the mistaken impression that if they paint their case, they'll do an awful job. You can do a great job of painting your case without spending a lot of money. By following a few simple steps, you will see that you can do this easily. As long as you have some free time, you can paint like a pro with a spray can.

Whether you have several thousand dollars in professional equipment or are using a $10 spray can, the basics are the same. How good a job you do depends solely on how well you've prepared for the job.

Here's what you'll need to get started:

- Respirator
- Rubber gloves
- Sandpaper
- Sanding block
- Sandable primer
- Paint color of your choice
- Rubbing compound
- Soap

Each item in the list deserves a bit more detail to help you make an informed purchase.

- **Respirator.** This device is not cheap (usually $30 to $200, depending on features), but your lungs will thank you for it. The price of a respirator depends on whether the respirator covers your entire face or just your nose and mouth. It's reusable, but the filters need regular replacement. I recommend investing in a full-face model to protect your eyes from paint fumes. If you do not use a full-face model respirator, you should still have proper eye protection.

- **Rubber gloves.** You'll need gloves to protect your hands from the paint and solvent, and to protect the painting surface from the oils on your hands. Rubber gloves cost approximately $5 for a package of 100.

- **Sandpaper.** Be sure to purchase the wet/dry variety. The grits you'll use are 400, 600, 1,000, 1,500, and 2,000. Sandpaper has an average cost of $3 to $6 per package of five sheets.

- **Sanding block.** These blocks can be made of either hard rubber or foam and have varying levels of flexibility. They typically cost $5 to $20.

- **Sandable primer.** Be sure to use the same brand of primer and paint. The primer can cost anywhere from $4 to $10, depending on whether you're using an automotive brand.

- **Paint color of your choice.** Use the same brand of paint as your primer. Typical cost is $3 to $10.

- **Rubbing compound.** This product is used to remove the fine sanding marks from the paint. Rubbing compound costs about $20.

- **Soap.** Use any mild dishwashing detergent to wash your case before you paint it. A clean surface will better hold the paint. I prefer to use Plastic Prep, which is made specifically for preparing plastic for painting. You should be able to purchase Plastic Prep for about $10.

Painting consists of three simple steps: sanding, painting, and finishing. Your work area should have a good water supply and plenty of ventilation. You'll also want a clean, dust-free area to help minimize the amount of sanding you'll need to do during the finishing stage. All sanding referred to here is wet sanding.

As with any project, always practice good safety habits. Wear proper clothing and eye protection. If you don't have experience in performing some of these preparation and painting tasks, find someone with experience to help you.

Now it's time for the first step: sanding the original paint, as shown in Figure 3.4.

3.4 Sanding the original paint.

Preparation is by far the most important step. By using 400-grit sandpaper in conjunction with the sanding block, you will make the dull and uneven finish on your case as smooth as satin. See Figure 3.5.

3.5 After sanding the original paint.

Sand the case with even strokes in the same direction across the entire case. This helps minimize scratches that might show through the finish. Depending on the color of your case, you might have trouble determining how smooth the surface is.

You do not need to completely sand through the original paint on the case. Just sand until the surface is smooth. After you've achieved the desired finish, wash the case with soap and water or with Plastic Prep and let it air dry.

Next, you need to apply the primer, as shown in Figure 3.6. The purpose of a primer is to seal the surface so the finish coat of paint will adhere, producing an even sheen.

> When using spray paint, place the can of paint in a bowl of warm water (not boiling) for a few minutes before painting. This warms up the paint, which thins it out and allows for the paint to atomize better. This makes thinner, smoother coats of paint easy.

3.6 Applying primer.

Before applying the primer, be sure to shake the can well. Stop painting every few minutes and shake the can. Paint with sandable primer and sand with 600-grit sandpaper after it has dried. Depending on the primer you use, drying time can take up to four hours. Wash the case with soap and water and let it air dry. Repeat the priming and sanding process until the surface is smooth and even. Be sure to follow the manufacturer's instructions concerning drying times.

Now you're ready for your paint color.

For best results, paint several thin coats rather than a single heavy coat. With your spray can raised about eight inches from the surface, use even strokes to apply the paint. Lightly mist the first layer, and then let this layer dry for 15–30 minutes. Apply another layer and let it dry. Repeat this process over the course of an hour until you have good color coverage. See Figure 3.7.

Don't worry about how thick the coat of paint is. Thinner is better, as long as it is even. You want to apply several thin coats. If you try to get a single thick coat, the paint might run. Also, remember that really thick paint chips or cracks more easily on flexible panels. Thinner paint will flex, allowing panels to flex naturally and not crack or chip the paint. Let the case dry for 24–48 hours (this is important).

Next, lightly wet sand the case with a 600-grit sandpaper until you have an even, smooth, satiny surface. Wash it with soap and water, and let it air dry. Repeat the painting and sanding process until you have no thin areas of color when sanded with 600-grit sandpaper. See Figure 3.8.

3.7 Painting the color.

3.8 Sanding the paint.

Before you start the final stage of sanding, you need to decide whether or not you can let the final coat of paint properly cure for 30 days. As paint cures, it also settles, causing the surface to distort and no longer be completely smooth.

Letting it cure at this stage will ensure that your finish stays as smooth as glass. If you don't wait, you will have to repaint the case to recapture that glasslike luster.

After you have let the paint cure for 30 days, and you have an even 600-grit surface with your color of choice, wet sand the case again using finer sandpaper, such as 1,000 grit. Wash the case. It is important that you wash the case between changing grits of sandpaper. If you don't, pieces of debris left over from the coarser sandpaper will scratch the surface. Continue this process until you reach 2,000 grit. See Figure 3.9. At this point, you'll see just how smooth the finish is going to look.

3.9 Repeat the sanding.

The next step in the process is to use the rubbing compound to remove the fine sanding marks. Follow with a swirl remover—a very fine finishing compound that removes the fine scratches from the rubbing compound—and you're done.

The rubbing compound you use should be designed for removing 2000-grit sanding marks; the swirl remover should remove up to 5000-grit sanding marks. If desired, you can then wax the case, but remember not to wax the case immediately. You must let the paint cure for at least 30 days before you wax it. The finish should be as smooth as glass. A smooth finish is especially easy to see with dark-colored finishes because scratching shows up very easily on them. See Figure 3.10.

3.10 Note the reflections in the black paint.

Project: Give Your Cell Phone Some Character and Pizzazz

Sure, modding your PC is cool, but how many people get to see it? Keep in mind that you can modify just about any type of case. This means you can also mod items you carry around with you every day. For example, why settle for a premade cell phone cover when you can paint your own design?

You'll first need a few items for this project:

- Masking tape
- Model paint (specifically for plastics)
- Plastic-model filler
- 400-grit sandpaper
- Dishwashing soap

Here are some tips specifically for painting cell phone covers:

1. Completely disassemble the phone. Paint and its fumes can damage the sensitive electronics. Carefully mask off any areas you don't want painted.

2. Use a paint that's designed for models. This paint is intended for use with plastics and will be the easiest to work with. Krylon Fusion works very well.

3. Preparation is the key to a good finish. Use plastic-model filler to fill in any nicks or areas you want smoothed out. Sand the cover with a 400-grit sandpaper and wash it thoroughly. Use dishwashing soap or a plastic cleaner that leaves no residue.

4. When painting, put the spray can in a bowl of warm water (not boiling) for a few minutes. This will help the paint atomize better.

5. Let the paint dry for at least 48 hours before using the cover. The longer you allow it to dry the better. Before the paint is fully cured, it is still soft and prone to damage. Total curing times vary. Most of the time it takes 30–60 days, but the phone is perfectly useable within that time. See Figure 3.11.

3.11 Kathy Cano Murillo, an artist from Phoenix, Arizona, posted this picture of her painted cell phone on her web site at www.craftychica.com. *(© Kathy Cano Murillo)*

Project: Open Box—Install a Window in Your Computer Case

One of the quickest and easiest modifications you can make to your computer case is to install a window. The window can be a simple shape, or you can go nuts and cut complex designs in the case.

Let's get to the tools you'll need:

- Drill
- Jigsaw, Dremel, or nibbler
- Utility knife
- Metal file
- Masking tape

You'll also need the window supplies:

- Acrylic or Lexan sheeting (1/8-inch thickness) can be purchased at most local hardware stores. I purchased mine at Home Depot (30 inches by 40 inches for $20; this will easily do multiple windows).
- You can also buy ready-made kits from suppliers such as PC Modifications or Xoxide.com. Most of these kits are less than $20.
- If you're creating your own design, you might need some sort of molding. I used DIY molding, which I purchased from PC Modifications. You can also use small colored hose cut lengthwise. It will fit snugly on the panel. Use silicon glue to glue it into place. In this type of application, you might want to glue the window on as well.

It's important to take the proper safety measures when handling power tools, so be sure to use goggles and ear protection. If you've never used these tools before, enlist the assistance of an experienced person. Improper handling and misuse of tools can result in serious injury.

Create the Window

The first step in designing your window is to sketch out what you want. I like to keep a notebook with all my ideas so I can refer to them when I need to.

Once you've figured out what you like, it's time for some handiwork. Put on your protective gear and get to work.

1. Use masking tape and lay out the design on the case to make sure your sketch will work. See Figure 3.12.

2. Mark the cut lines on the masking tape. I also like to use more tape to protect the surrounding areas of the case.

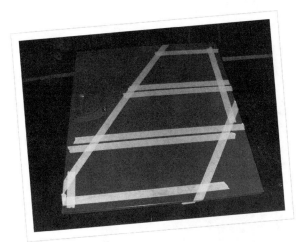

3.12 Lay out the design.

3. Drill a pilot hole for the jigsaw/nibbler, so that you have an edge in the middle of your panel from which you can start cutting. See Figure 3.13.

4. Cut out the hole. When using power tools, always use eye and ear protection.

3.13 Drill the pilot hole.

5. Use the file to remove any burs and also to remove any high spots or uneven cuts. See Figure 3.14.

6. Once the case has been cut, use the holes to mark the acrylic, as shown in Figure 3.15. The molding I used requires a gap. The molding comes with a washer to be used as a spacer for tracing the pattern on the window to be cut.

3.14 *Make your edges nice and smooth.*

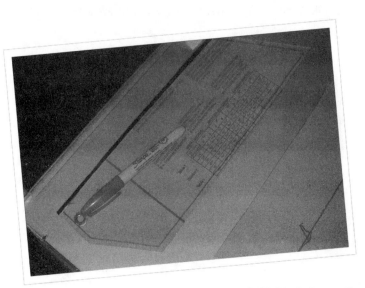

3.15 *Mark the acrylic.*

7. Cut your molding to fit the window.

8. Install the window. The molding holds the window in place. See Figure 3.16.

3.16 The molding holds the window in place.

If you do not use this type of molding, you have a couple of options for fastening the window to the case. You could glue it in place. If so, allow extra material that will not be seen from the outside for the glue to be applied to. You could also use bolts or rivets. I personally prefer to use glue unless the bolts are part of the exterior visual design of the mod.

9. Sit back and enjoy. See Figure 3.17.

3.17 This mod combined painting and windows for a unique look.

Project: The TechTV PC Case

When a mod calls for extreme precision and power, sometimes you need to bring out the big guns.

I love all the mods I've made with the tools in my home studio, but there's only so much you can accomplish by hand. If you want to graduate to the big leagues, you need to bring out the heavy hitters: lasers. You won't do this at home, but we contacted Precision Laser Cutting and recruited their help in creating a special TechTV PC case.

The whole process was painless. I came up with a design for a case with the TechTV logo and the new logo for "The Screen Savers." My original design was much too complicated (2,000 plus individual shapes to cut), so the guys at Precision Laser helped me clean it up by eliminating the lines that didn't work and removing extra lines and overlapping cuts. We were then ready to start zapping.

There is something very cool about watching a 5,000-watt laser cut through steel like it was tissue paper. The waterjet cutting is equally impressive. How many times do you get to see water being pumped through 100-horsepower compressors and boosted up to 55,000 psi?

Table 3.1 describes the differences between laser cutting and water cutting. This information is based on material found on the Tesko Laser web site.

> We just want to say a special thanks again to Dave and Rich at Precision Laser Cutting. They were very patient with our crew who would repeatedly ask, "Can you do that one more time?"

Table 3.1

Laser Cutting versus Water Cutting

Laser Cutting	Water Cutting
Energy source	
Gas laser (carbon dioxide)	High-pressure water pump
Typical uses	
Cutting, drilling, engraving, ablation, structuring, welding	Cutting, ablation, structuring
Materials able to be cut	
All metals (excluding highly reflective metals), all plastics, glass, and wood	All materials
Material thickness	
~0.12-inch to 0.4-inch, depending on material	~0.4-inch to six inches
Common applications	
Cutting flat sheet steel for sheet metal processing	Cutting stone, ceramics, and metals of greater thickness
Minimum size of cutting slit	
0.006-inch, depending on cutting speed	0.02-inch
Initial investment	
$300,000 with a 20 kW pump and a 6.5-foot by 4-foot table	$750,000 or more

Project: Give the Window to Your Computer's Soul a Unique Look

Windows on PCs are now very popular. No, I'm not talking about a particular operating system. I'm talking about an actual window on a computer case. Case windows are popping up everywhere, either as case customizations done by modders or on pre-modded cases.

Modders take pride in making a case look unique. That means doing more than just installing a plain old clear window. The window should reflect your personality. Let's look at some techniques to enhance your case windows.

> Some of these case enhancement techniques involve power tools, so you'll need goggles and ear protection.

But first, a few special trimmings are needed:

- Appliqués
- Dremel tool (for etching acrylic)
- Marker
- Rubbing alcohol
- Lights
- Tints
- Baby shampoo
- Squeegee
- Hair dryer
- File
- Decals

> If you find you need additional help, visit my forums at `http://yoshi.us` and post a message.

Appliqués and Etchings

Appliqués are decals you can apply to your window and are available from a number of retailers. To find appliqué vendors, just do a Google search on PC appliqués or use a similar term.

Because most windows are made of acrylic, you can also forgo the appliqués and etch your image directly onto the window if you'd like. It might sound a bit risky and complicated, but it's actually quite simple:

1. Print your design. This will be used as your template.

2. Tape the template under the window and use it as a guide. See Figure 3.18. Instead of printing a template, you can also draw directly on the window using a marker.

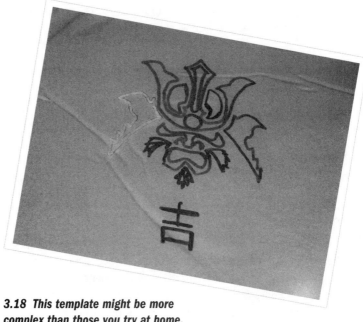

3.18 This template might be more complex than those you try at home.

3. Etch the image by following your template. I like to use a Dremel tool with a small round bur.

4. If you use a marker to draw directly on the window, you can use rubbing alcohol to erase the remaining ink.

Fortunately, acrylic isn't expensive. Most window-size pieces cost under $20. Keep in mind that this is an art project, so don't feel limited by your template. Embellish your etching by adding texture and details. If you ruin the acrylic, just buy another piece and start over.

Lights

What's not to like about acrylic windows? As discussed earlier, acrylic is easy to etch, it's affordable, and of course, it's translucent. You knew that, but here's something you might not know.

If you install a light on the *edge* of an etched acrylic window, the etched area glows the color of the light. And you can have only the etching illuminated when the system is powered on.

In addition, you can get creative with your lighting. You can use a multicolored setup with multiple layers of acrylic, each with its own design and color. You can also play with shapes.

> **Make sure you keep the light from escaping around the edge of the window. This is especially important if you're using multiple layers with different colors. Remember, the light inside the case (neon, LED, etc.) will also show up in the etched surface.**
>
> **In my case, I used LEDs that are about as thick as the window. I also used black electrical tape to isolate the light.**

Tints

You can also use window tints to enhance your lights, either by changing the color or by helping to create the illusion of a solid surface when there is no light showing through. Mask off the area you want to keep clear. Paint the window the same color as the tint. After it dries, apply the window tint. The tint will make the panel look solid when the computer is shut off. When you power on your computer, the lights will show your window detail.

Cut the window tint into the desired shape and apply it to the window. Sound hard? Don't worry. With a little practice it's no sweat. Here are a few tips:

1. Use a mixture of baby shampoo and water (mostly water) and spray it on the window and tint film. This helps ensure that no part will immediately stick. Use a squeegee to remove the liquid that is trapped under the tinting film, so that no air pockets are trapped under the film. Start from the middle of the window, so that you're pushing the air pockets and the liquid out. If you have any dust or air under the tint, it won't look right.

2. Use a hair dryer to dry the film as you squeegee out the liquid. The hair dryer dries the tint and activates the glue. The heat will cause the glue to bond to the window with more strength.

3. If you're covering the entire window with tint, use a fine file to smooth out the edge. Apply the tint so it extends beyond the edge of the window. Then file the edge. This allows the tint to cover the very edge of the window.

Painting

Another fun technique is to paint part of the window. You can paint the area you don't want visible and leave the rest clear.

Decals

Decals are similar to appliqués. Most of the decals you'll find are frosted to look like etchings, but you can also use solid decals. The choice is yours.

You can visit your local sign store to obtain ready-to-apply (RTA) decals made to your specifications. In most instances, you can provide the store with a digital file of the graphic you want, and the store will make a decal for you.

Project: Light Up Your Case

With so many options for lighting available these days, it's possible to be extremely creative. Don't limit yourself to simply adding a light inside your case. Use the lighting to enhance certain areas or to add special effects to graphics you have created, such as window etchings. I'll discuss three lighting categories: light emitting diodes (LEDs), neon, and electroluminescent wire (EL). Each has its own strengths.

LEDs

LEDs have a focused area of light that can be very good for highlighting a component or adding light to a window etching without lighting up the rest of the case. You can use individual LEDs, ones that come in prebuilt clusters, or even ones with built-in controllers. LEDs are very cheap, have extremely low power consumption, generate very little heat, and have a very long life span.

Lazer LED

Lazer LEDs range from $13.99–17.99 and are made to plug into your computer. They come with a prewired Molex connector and are mounted in a block that contains the three LEDs. Each side light is angled at 45 degrees from the center light to spread the light more evenly. Lazer LEDs are a nice option because they install in less than a minute. Lazer LEDs come in red, green, and blue as well as multicolored and ultraviolet (UV). For more information, visit **www.xoxide.com/lazerled.html**.

MADLights

MADLights gave me a first look at its new product ($59.95), which takes a series of LEDs and the company's custom controller to make animated lighting sequences. Hooking them up is easy. Each kit contains four 18-inch leads with red, green, and blue LEDs on them, two switches with 24-inch leads, and a controller board. The switches control the program and speed. They work quite well. The length of the leads allows them to be placed far apart, letting you customize your lighting theme to suit your taste. To mount the switches requires drilling two holes. The kit comes with mounting tabs with double-sided tape for the controller board and LED leads. MADLights is a well thought-out product and proves to be a good value for what you get. For more information, visit **www.madlights.com**.

Neon: Cold Cathode Lights

Neon lights have been around for a while. The idea to add neon lights to computers could have been inspired by what people saw in Times Square or hanging from the window of the local pub. Either way, neon lights are a cheap, easy mod. Cold cathodes are available in a variety of colors; they even come in multicolored and UV varieties. One of the newest additions to neon lighting for modding is cold cathodes mounted to fans. They are very useful for lighting the interior of a case because they are typically very bright. For more information, visit `www.xoxide.com/coldcathodes.html`.

Electroluminescent Lighting

Cool Neon makes a unique form of lighting. It is a flexible phosphorescent wire that glows very bright when current is applied to it. It is also known as EL wire. This product is good for uses that require lighting specific complex shapes. It can be bent, twisted, or manipulated to suit your needs. It can be used in any length up to 330 inches, depending on the driver unit you use. Cool Neon also makes a flat light called FLAT Lamp. For more information, visit `www.coolneon.com`.

FLAT Lamp

FLAT Lamp works on the same principle as the EL wire, but it is just 3-inches wide and 0.01-inch thick. That's about as thick as a heavy weight paper. FLAT Lamp can be cut shorter, but unlike the EL wire, you can't resolder the remaining pieces.

Project: Blink Blink

Now that you are committed to modding your case, how about adding a display that can show your vital PC stats, Winamp information, game stats, stock tickers, news tickers, and much more? There are many functional reasons to add a liquid crystal display (LCD) to your case. But let's face it, the reason we do mods is simply because it's cool.

This is a very easy mod. There are two parts, the hardware installation and the software configuration.

Hardware

A variety of manufacturers produce LCD and vacuum fluorescent displays (VFDs). I chose a Matrix Orbital VFD2041, which you can find out more about at www.matrixorbital.com. I wanted a display that was very bright and that could display a good amount of information at one time.

Here are some other places to find displays:

- Crystal Fontz (www.crystalfontz.com)
- Seetron (www.seetron.com)
- EIO (www.eio.com)

EIO has cheap prices, but inventory changes frequently so you have to keep checking if you're looking for something specific.

How you mount your LCD display is up to you. External cases are an option, but I chose to build mine into the case. I used an Antec 6030B. I decided that it should be mounted in the front of the case, which limited where to mount it because of the door. The grill in the front looked like a good candidate for mounting, however. Mounting the VFD required removing some or all of the entire grill. After careful consideration, I removed the entire grill, which gave me the cosmetic effect I wanted. To fill the void of the grill, I used a plastic panel that framed the VFD and provided ventilation to the case fans.

Here are the supplies I used for this project:

- VFD display
- 1/8-inch acrylic
- Black spray paint
- Serial cable
- Floppy power cable

Mounting the VFD

The following steps were used to mount the VFD:

1. Cut the existing grill out of the front of the case using a Dremel.
2. Take careful measurements of the empty space and cut out an acrylic blank to fit in place.
3. Use the 5-inch bay door to trace the curve to be cut in the top and bottom of the blank.
4. Decide on the location of the VFD, and then carefully lay it in place to measure the size of the mask for painting.
5. Cut the VFD's mask and place it into position on the backside of the plastic blank.
6. With the mask in place, use several thin coats of black paint.
7. After the paint has dried for 48 hours, remove the mask.
8. Mark the layout for the case fans' ventilation holes.
9. Use a drill press to drill out the ventilation holes.
10. With that done, use another piece of plastic (from a CD jewel case) to make a mounting bracket for the VFD.
11. To cut the jewel case, score it with a utility knife and break it along the cut line.
12. Bend the plastic by heating the plastic to make it nice and pliable (not too hot or it will melt and distort). Using two pieces of thin wood to keep the bend straight, carefully bend the plastic to the desired shape. Hold in place until the plastic cools a little and hardens.
13. Hold the mounting bracket in place with small machine screws.
14. Once the bracket is finished, mount the plastic cover.
15. Lay the cover in place and secure it with a few small drops of silicon glue.
16. Connect your serial cable and power leads, and you are done.

Software

There are a lot of LCD controls and plug-ins available on the market. Finding the one best suited for your application can be a matter of trying several different options. Valuable sources of information and advice are available on the many message boards and forums. If you don't find the answer you are looking for, post a new thread to ask your question, and it will most likely be answered. Here are two sites I would recommend:

- Hardforum (www.hardforum.com)
- Matrix Orbital (www.lcdforums.com)

I had a few requirements for the software I used:

- Compatibility with Winamp to display song information
- Compatibility with Mother Board Monitor
- Ability to customize the interface

The software I chose to use was LCDriver. It gets information from Winamp and Mother Board Monitor, and it will even tell you when you have new email. It is not a free program ($15 after a 30-day trial period), but it has the nicest interface in my opinion. Setup is simple once you read the Getting Started page. You decide what information you want, where it goes, and how long to display it. If you are so inclined, you can even develop your own plug-ins for it.

To obtain some free programs, check out the following products and web sites:

- LCD4Linux (http://lcd4linux.sourceforge.net)
- LCDPROC (http://lcdproc.omnipotent.net)
- LCDriver (http://lcdriver.pointofnoreturn.org)
  Version 2.0 is currently not available for download.
- LCDSmartie (http://backupteam.gamepoint.net/smartie/)
- LCDC (www.lcdc.cc/index.php)

Chapter 4

Modifying Drives

It's time to dump that drab and dreary hard-drive case for something you can see through. In this chapter, I'll explain how to make a see-through hard-drive case. Others have done this mod many times, but I want to add my special touch to it.

Yoshi's Mods: Project Specularis

Putting a window in a hard drive can be a very expensive endeavor. But this is a fun mod, and it's not too complicated. That said, you still need to be careful. I recommend using an older hard drive that you don't care about very much. Older hard drives also seem to handle the mod with fewer problems.

> As with every mod, if you don't have experience using cutting tools, don't use them. Have an experienced person assist you. And of course, always wear eye protection.

Here's what you'll need:

- **Hard drive.** An older hard drive will work nicely.
- **Clear acrylic or Lexan sheeting.** A thickness of 0.020-inch works well.
- **Epoxy.** Use an extended-work-time variety that sets in 30 minutes.
- **Dremel tool (or clone).** Use with the following accessories:
  - Cut-off disc
  - Carbide cutter
- **Utility knife and No. 10 X-acto knife.** Be sure to have plenty of new blades on hand for both.
- **Drill and drill bits.** A drill press is preferred because it's safer and more accurate, but a hand drill will suffice. If you've been thinking about picking up a drill press, here's your excuse.
- **Needle files.** Very small files for cleaning up corners or small details. Or if your budget will allow it, spring for some diamond needle files.
- **400-grit sandpaper.** Use to prepare the gluing surface.
- **Torqx driver set.** Almost all hard drives use Torqx fasteners.

Construction Instructions

Now it's time to get to work.

1. Take the drive apart, as shown in Figure 4.1. But be very careful.

   · If you have access to a clean room, great. Use it.

   · Otherwise, use a clean, dust-free area.

   · Use a clean (preferably new) Tupperware or similar container to store the drive while you complete the rest of the mod.

4.1 Drive with cover removed.

2. Plan your cuts. Use a grease pencil to sketch the cuts on the drive cover, as shown in Figure 4.2. A grease pencil allows you to wipe off the marks and start over if the cut marks are not to your liking.

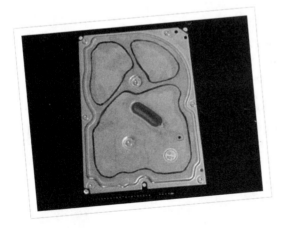

4.2 Mark your cuts with a grease pencil.

- Consider the holes for the platter/spindle support and head/actuator mounts. This was the source of problems on one of my drives because I left the actuator without a mount on the top cover. As a result, it caused the heads to contact the data area of the drive, destroying it.

- Because the actuator is small and light, I assumed that the bottom mount would suffice. This worked fine on older drives, but not on new drives.

- However, because every cloud has a silver lining, I used the motor and platters from the destroyed drive to make a really sweet fan.

3. Cut out the holes.

- If you're doing a basic square cut, you can make your cuts exactly.

- Use a Dremel tool with cut-off discs to carefully cut out the hole.

- Use a fine-tooth file to clean up the cut.

- If you're cutting a complex shape, as shown in Figure 4.3, cut a little beyond your markings, leaving a small amount of excess material so you have more flexibility when cleaning it up.

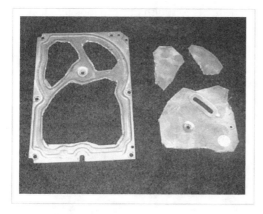

4.3 Rough cut of design.

4. Using the drive cover as a template, trace out the window on the acrylic.

5. Using the utility knife or No. 10 blade, cut out the window. Remember to cut it a little beyond your markings, leaving some excess material so you can fine-tune it before installation. Line it up with the cover and fine-tune it as necessary. See Figure 4.4.

6. On the window cutout, mark the holes that will be needed for mounting the cover and drill them out.

7. Lightly sand the cover around the area where the window will be attached. You want to give the epoxy a good surface to adhere to.

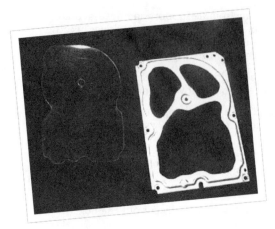

4.4 Finished cutout.

8. Glue the window in place. Use a thin, even layer of epoxy.

   • Use an extended-work-time epoxy so it doesn't set before you get the window in place.

   • Use the epoxy sparingly. The glue tends to squish out and look ugly if you use too much.

9. Clean both sides of the new cover thoroughly and reassemble the drive. See Figure 4.5.

4.5 Another completed hard-drive mod.

Project: Stealth CD-ROM

For novice modders, this is an easy mod to begin with, and it is completely reversible. Making a stealth CD-ROM drive is not new; people have been doing it for quite a while. It is also one of the simplest and quickest mods you can do.

Almost all of the supplies you will need come with your computer case. If you have plastic bay covers, as shown in Figure 4.6, this mod should take no more than 10 minutes. If you have a metal case, it will not take much longer, but might require a Dremel or other type of rotary cutting tool.

Here's what you'll need:

- Plastic bay covers
- Double-sided foam tape
- Dremel or other rotary tool, or utility knife

4.6 Drives before the stealth mod.

1. Find the drive bay covers that came with your case. Hopefully, you still have them. Take a look at the back of the bay cover and decide what you want to keep and what you want to remove. See Figure 4.7. I like to take everything off except the very front surface, so the cover is as thin as possible.

2. Cut off any surplus material. You can use diagonal cutters or a Dremel. You can even use a utility knife. But no matter what type of tool you use, be very careful.

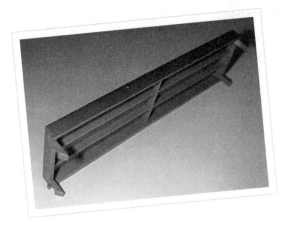

4.7 Back of the bay cover.

3. Use the double-sided foam tape to secure the bay cover. Put the tape on the drive, as shown in Figure 4.8. Then place the bay cover over the drive and press it into place, as shown in Figure 4.9. The tape should allow the cover to bend enough so that the Eject button can be pressed. You might have to glue a small spacer onto the cover if there is a gap between the cover and the button. I like to use a piece of pencil eraser as a spacer.

4.8 Double-sided foam tape on drive.

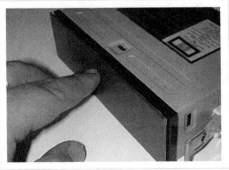

4.9 Stealth bay cover mounted on drive.

4. Slide the drive back into the case so the new stealth drive is flush with the front of the case. See Figure 4.10.

4.10 The closed stealth drive.

5. You can be as creative as you like with this mod. For example, you can also cut out holes for the activity LED. Or, if you want to paint your computer case, you can be even more creative because this mod provides you with additional real estate to paint on.

The completed mod is shown in Figure 4.11.

4.11 Opening the drive.

Chapter 5

Modding Gadgets

Inspiration for projects can come from a variety of web sites; one I frequent is Metku Mods at www.metku.net. The modifications on this site are, for the most part, cheap and simple. Most anyone can do them, and they're also cool. In this chapter, I'll explain how to do one of the mods from the site.

Project Iris: Mousing Around

The mod at Metku Mods that inspired me for this project was the FireWheel—a mouse mod that produces an illuminated transparent mouse wheel. I wanted to do one of my own, but add two colors of light instead of one. So, I decided to change the bottom LED to blue instead of red.

For this project, I used the following supplies:

- USB optical mouse
- 5v red LED
- 3.7v blue LED
- 24-gauge solid wire
- Heat-shrink tubing
- 1/4-inch acrylic or Lexan plastic
- Super glue and de-bonder

The total cost for the project was $40. The mouse was $30, LEDs were $4, plastic was $5, and the heat-shrink tubing was $1. The wire and glue I had lying around (it runs about $8 if you need to buy it).

The mouse I chose to use was a Kensington Optical Elite. I chose it because it had a blue LED already installed, shining at the wheel.

A few tools are also needed to complete this project:

- Phillips screwdriver #1
- Soldering iron and solder

- Hand drill or drill press (preferred)
- Dremel tool
- Medium file
- Sandpaper, medium (180–400 grit)
- Multimeter (optional but recommended)

Remember to always wear proper eye protection when performing a mod.

Project Instructions

Let's get started.

1. Disassemble the mouse. A mouse is usually held together by screws, which are sometimes under the sliders, as shown in Figure 5.1. You will be working with the main circuit board and the wheel.

5.1 Disassemble the mouse.

Small screws can also be hidden behind stickers.

2. Desolder the existing red LED points, as shown in Figure 5.2, and solder the blue 3.7v LED in its place. Be sure to pay attention to the polarity or the LED will not work.

5.2 Desolder the red LED.

3. Cover the leads of the LED with heat-shrink tubing, leaving enough room to solder the 24-gauge wire. See Figure 5.3.

5.3 LED leads covered with heat-shrink tubing.

4. Solder the red LED leads onto the underside of the board, as shown in Figure 5.4. I used the 5Vdc that comes from the USB line. The LED will be on the whole time the computer is on and the mouse is plugged in.

5.4 Solder points for the red LED leads.

5. Remove the rubber ring from the wheel. Place the wheel's shaft in a drill or Dremel tool, as shown in Figure 5.5. Use a file or rough sandpaper to remove the ridge from the wheel while it is spinning. This is essentially a homemade lathe. You only need to remove one of the ridges. Be careful because the plastic spindle can break if you use too much force.

5.5 Mouse wheel spindle mounted on the Dremel with lip removed from one side.

6. Cut out a piece of plastic a little bit bigger than you need, as shown in Figure 5.6. You need to be able to hold it down securely (a clamp is recommended) while drilling. A drill press will produce the best results if you have access to one, but for our purposes a hand drill will work fine. Using a 0.5-inch plastic drill bit, drill out the center of the new wheel.

5.6 0.5-inch hole (drill is not actually running).

Clamp your workpiece to the table. Do not hold the piece in your hand when drilling it. Keep your hands away from the drill bit.

7. Use the rubber ring from the wheel to trace a rough outline of the new wheel. Line up the two pieces using the 0.5-inch holes. See Figure 5.7.

5.7 Rubber ring with plastic that will be used for replacement ring.

8. Use your Dremel tool with a cut-off disc to cut out the wheel. Don't cut the wheel too small; it's easier to remove the excess material from a wheel that's too big. Remember, you can't add material if you cut it too small. If you have access to a band saw or scroll saw, all the better. Don't worry if the wheel is not perfectly round at this point. See Figure 5.8.

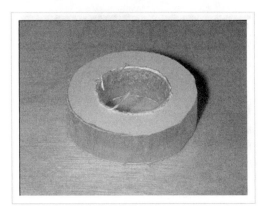

5.8 Rough cutout of the clear, plastic wheel.

9. Using a couple drops of Superglue, place the plastic wheel on the drill bit near the shaft where it is smooth, as shown in Figure 5.9.

5.9 Rough-cut wheel mounted on the drill bit.

10. Spin the piece in your drill, using the file as a cutting tool. See Figure 5.10. The high spots will be cut first, truing the roundness of the piece. Once it is round and the basic shape is correct, use sandpaper to smooth it while spinning it in the drill.

5.10 Wheel is shaped while spinning it on the drill press.

11. Remove the wheel from the drill bit using de-bonder. Use the Dremel to adjust the size of the inside hole of the mouse wheel to fit the spindle. See Figure 5.11. If you are careful and work slowly, you will be able to install the wheel on the spindle without using glue.

5.11 Fine-tuning the inside diameter of the wheel.

12. Install the circuit board, wheel, and other parts. You can now enjoy your illuminated mouse, as shown in Figure 5.12.

5.12 The final product.

Project: Cooling a Mouse?

I recently received an email suggesting this project. Actually, I won't really be cooling the mouse, but instead will be cooling your hand while using the mouse. If you spend a lot of time using your computer, you might get sweaty palms from the lack of airflow between your hand and the mouse. Well, it's easy enough to fix that.

Here's what you'll need:

- Mouse
- Fan
- Soldering iron and solder
- 24-gauge wire
- Drill and drill bits
- Double-sided tape (thick foam kind)
- LED (optional)
- Resistor (optional)

I suggest using a USB mouse because it has ample 5Vdc power. A PS2 mouse can also be used, but you will need to use a multimeter to find the appropriate power lead.

Fans can be found in a variety of places. As a matter of fact, I used an old video card fan. You might want to go to your local used computer store and ask if you can dig through discarded parts to salvage a fan. Most of the time, the store owners will let you do this for free or at least for just a buck or two.

To calculate the correct resistance for your LED so it doesn't burn out, visit `www.bit-tech.net/article/68`. To calculate resistance manually, use Ohm's law, which is $V=IR$. Solving for R yields $R=V/I$. V is voltage in volts, I is current in amps, and R is resistance in ohms. V is the difference between the supplied voltage and the required voltage. Because we're using milliamps instead of amps, we also need to multiply by 1000.

In addition, because we're using the difference between supplied voltage and required LED voltage, we need to subtract. So the formula becomes $R=$(*Supplied volts - LED voltage required*)/(*current in milliamps*)*1000*.

Steps to Cool Down

After you have all your supplies, you're ready to begin.

1. Open the mouse and remove all its parts, leaving an empty shell. You should be able to do this without using any tools.

2. Use a pencil to mark your pattern for the vent holes. I suggest drilling some inlet holes as well on the bottom and sides of the mouse. If nothing else, it can help tie in the design of the pattern on the top of the mouse.

3. Use the drill to carefully drill out the required holes. Go back by hand (not with the drill) with a larger bit to chamfer the holes.

4. Solder a couple of extensions onto the corresponding USB pins (red is 5Vdc and black is ground, but use a multimeter to test these first). I used the bottom points, which are already soldered.

5. If you are installing an LED, solder the resistor to the LED first. Wire it in series to the longer side of the LED.

6. Cut the fan out of the housing, leaving just the blades and backing.

7. Attach your power leads to the fan and LED.

8. Use the double-sided tape to attach the fan to the top of the mouse. The backing of the fan goes toward the shell.

9. Ensure that no wires come in contact with the moving fan blades.

10. Reassemble the mouse and you're done.

Project: Orpheus

I love listening to music. But I don't like changing CDs. So, I thought, why not build an MP3 player that will give me the sonic quality I desire. While I'm at it, why not make it controllable by a WiFi-enabled Pocket PC. And why not put it in a case that looks like it belongs in an Audiophile stereo rack.

It should be a simple task: cut up a few pieces of wood, plastic, and metal (see Figure 5.13), bolt everything together, and enjoy. Well it's not quite that easy, but it's not very complicated either.

5.13 Yoshi cutting metal on the table saw.

Software

Choosing the software for this project was not an easy decision. There are many reasons to run Linux as the OS for an MP3 Jukebox. But unfortunately, the sound card I used—M-Audio Audiophile 2496—didn't have any Linux drivers.

That left me with Windows. Because there are many plug-ins available for Winamp, I decided to use it. I found a plug-in called BrowseAmp at `www.thasler.de`. It has a basic interface, which was a bonus because I would be using it with a Pocket PC.

BrowseAmp also allows you to make your own HTML pages. This enabled me to tailor the interface page to fit the Pocket PC. I left most of the features of the base HTML page in place; I resized everything to 304 x 168, which is a good viewing size for the Pocket PC. I also removed the title, bit rate, and other nonessential features.

I put Winamp in the Startup directory so that it would load on startup. And I used LCDC in conjunction with my Matrix Orbital VFD2041 display to show the current track playing.

Hardware

The hardware items I used in this project include the following components:

- **Motherboard.** Epia Mini ITX 800 MHz
- **Sound card.** M-Audio Audiophile 2496
- **DVD.** Pioneer Slot Loading
- **Hard drive.** Western Digital Special Edition 120GB with an 8MB buffer
- **Vacuum Fluorescent Display (VFD).** Matrix Orbital VFD2041
- **Power supply.** Antec 300w

Basically, this small desktop PC has a motherboard, CPU, hard drive, DVD, power supply, cooling fan, USB interface device, remote mouse and keyboard, and a case. The case of course is not available off the shelf, and a few of the other components had to be modified. The case was designed to look like a top-quality stereo component. This meant I had to make some modifications to certain parts of it to make everything work.

I first had to figure out what my final dimensions would be. In keeping with the stereo motif, I went with the dimensions of 17 inches wide, 14 inches deep, and 5 inches tall. This presented the problem of having to make the standard power supply fit in the case with ample room for airflow. To solve the problem, I took the power supply out of its case. I decided that if I was going to build the case, why not have the power jack mounted in the case instead of the power supply; so this solution had two benefits.

Once the dimensions were decided, I had to mock up a layout. Using a piece of cardboard as a guide for my dimensions, I laid out the parts to see how much room I would have.

I chose the Via Epia Mini ITX motherboard because it is 170mm x 170mm with onboard video and Ethernet. Once the layout was complete, I removed the extraneous power lines from the power supply and shortened the leads on the others to fit the case. I wanted it to look nice as well as function properly.

> If you try this mod, be sure to leave enough wire for the path it will be secured into. Also, take into account the airflow when deciding on the cable routing.

I used a large fan that spins at 1700 rpm to reduce noise yet keep a good airflow.

I also used aluminum sheeting to make the mounting chassis. For the front and top panels, I used 1/4-inch Plexiglas with a smoke tint because I wanted to see what was inside. I went with wood on the sides because I have always liked the look of audio equipment that incorporated wood. Figure 5.14 shows the finished case before the components were installed.

Once everything was done, I had to do some last minute fitting of pieces that were not quite to spec, but it all worked out. I am enjoying it immensely.

5.14 The finished case without the components.

Project: Faraday

Most of the new PDAs come with built-in rechargeable batteries. But older PDAs such as Palm Pilots or Handspring Visors can easily be switched over to use rechargeable batteries as well.

A couple of disclaimers before we begin:

- If you decide to open up your PDA and modify it, be prepared for the fact that you might destroy it, and you will void your warranty if you still have one.

- This is a very simple charging design without a voltage regulator. However, it is possible to overcharge your batteries and in doing so damage your PDA, although I have consistently left mine connected for 4–7 hours without a problem.

When doing this project, I found it to be very cheap and easy. The total cost was under $10.

Here is what I used:

- 10-ohm resistor ($0.20)
- Two 1N914 diodes ($0.34)
- Two AAA NiMH rechargeable batteries ($8)
- Heat-shrink tubing ($0.40)
- Soldering iron and solder
- Small Phillips screwdriver
- Small wire cutters

Let's begin the project.

1. Take the Visor apart. Actually, you only need to remove the button board, so stop there.
2. Take the cradle apart.

3. Modding the cradle is really easy because solder points already exist. Solder the 10-ohm resistor in the cradle. Install it between TP1 and TP4. This gives 5Vdc to pin 7. See Figure 5.15.

5.15 Soldering points in the cradle.

4. On the button board, shown in Figure 5.16, take the 1N914 diodes and solder them in series between pin 7 and the positive battery terminal. Note the polarity of the diodes when installing them. Use the heat-shrink tubing to cover them so nothing shorts out. You might need to cut out a little bit of the plastic surrounding the battery compartment to accommodate the diode's wire.

5. Put everything back together and install your batteries.

5.16 The button board.

> Do not put the Visor in its cradle without batteries installed, you will damage it.

Altogether, it took me about 20 minutes to complete this mod, and it was very easy. By the way, you can still use regular batteries in your PDA and connect it to a noncharging cradle without a problem.

Chapter 6

Yoshi's Boxx

What makes for a great gaming experience? Is it all about the raw numbers a system has? I don't think so. It's about what we see. We are by nature visual beings, so we like to make our environment aesthetically pleasing.

Videogame Console or Work of Art?

If you're like me, you prefer minimalist aesthetics. How much do you think is too much: one, three, six boxes cluttering your desktop, all of them distinctly different visually? Why not mount all of those systems into one box?

With Yoshi's Boxx, shown in Figure 6.1, I bridged the divide between form and function. The Boxx provides a single physical portal for videogames.

6.1 Yoshi's Boxx.

The Vision

I had been thinking about a project like this for a while, so I decided to tear apart a few systems I had lying around and compact them into one case.

The following systems are installed in the Boxx:

- Atari 2600
- Nintendo Entertainment System (8-bit)
- Microsoft Xbox
- Nintendo GameCube
- Sony PlayStation 2
- A custom PC

Planning Yoshi's Boxx

Before I could even start working things out in my head, I had to take everything apart and get an idea of the dimensions I would be working with.

This isn't as easy as it sounds. Some of the systems use Torqx bolts, so I needed more than a Phillips screwdriver. The Nintendo GameCube uses something like a reverse Torqx bolt (GameBit 4.5mm) to hold it together. But I didn't have a tool for these types of bolts, so I used a left-hand drill bit and drilled the bolts out. (I wouldn't be needing them again anyway.)

> If you don't have Torqx-brand wrenches, it's a good idea to purchase a set. You will use them again, I promise. I've accumulated many good tools over the years, but these are essential to a well-stocked modder's tool chest.

While in the process of disassembling these machines, many fluorescent stickers glowered at me with threatening warnings about voiding my warranties. With thorough disregard, I did it anyway. And now a brief message from our lawyers: "When disregarding warranty warnings, proceed at your own risk."

Once I'd determined the dimensions I would work with, I wrote down each measurement, made some sketches, and then wrote up a parts list. For me, it helps a lot to see my plans in writing before I jump from the proverbial frying pan into the fire. See Figure 6.2.

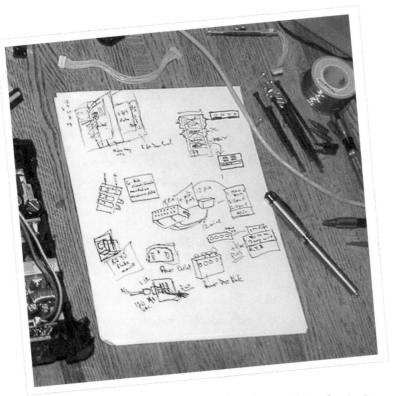

6.2 Sketches and ideas for the Boxx.

Take the time to sit back and think about your plans. Talk to your friends about what you want to do. Other peoples' perspectives can be invaluable. I have the great benefit of having many talented friends and coworkers (thanks guys). Once you think the whole project through from start to finish, tuck it away for at least a day. I personally couldn't stop thinking about my plans, even though they were not in front of me. When I returned to the project, there were many aspects that I had thought about that needed fine-tuning. I guarantee that when you come back to your project, you will have thought of some detail(s) you originally forgot to incorporate or features that just would not work.

When I revisited my plans, I realized that I needed to clarify some of my modifications. How would I make the mounting brackets? How would I lay out the components in the box? Would I have enough airflow? How would I switch the audio and video? I may not be a master artist, but I better understood what was involved once I had put my plans on paper. Documenting your ideas will help you determine what will and will not work before it's too late. Draw, sketch, doodle, whatever—and save it all.

Game Consoles Dry Fit

After I worked everything out theoretically, I took the components and did a test run, trying to fit them together without cutting or mounting anything. Good thing I did. What looked good in my head and on paper simply wouldn't work in the real world.

> **Don't cut or mount anything before you double-check your layout. You're bound to regret it if you don't recheck your plans.**

Xbox

At first I thought the Xbox motherboard should go behind the PC motherboard, but no luck there. It wouldn't clear the side cover. Then I thought I should mount it under the top of the case, but that wouldn't work either. The connectors that attach to the Xbox motherboard, the Xbox, and the PC power supply prevented those fits. I finally decided to make a mounting plate that would sit above the PC motherboard and raise the edge to clear the PC components.

The placement of the Xbox power supply was a limiting factor because of the length of the power leads (unless you want to make an extension for these wires). Also, I had to consider that the Xbox Power and Eject buttons should be somewhere in the front of the case.

GameCube

The GameCube game CDs are inserted straight from the top of the unit. To include it in the Boxx, you must either manufacture a custom enclosure for the drive or leave the unit almost intact. I happily discovered that the system is almost 5.25 inches wide. A little work with a belt sander, and it should slide into place.

One obstacle I faced with the GameCube was the controller ports. They are attached with a ribbon cable that is not very common and is difficult to solder. The controller ports can be placed in front of the unit, so the ribbon cable doesn't require modification. But the stock ribbon cable is just barely long enough to fit.

PlayStation 2

Placing the PlayStation 2 was pretty straightforward. I found that it could easily be mounted beside the 5.25-inch drive bays if the power supply was relocated. All I had to do was carefully mark the cuts I would be making in the front of the box.

Nintendo Entertainment System

Mounting the 8-bit Nintendo system was an interesting dilemma. Its cartridges don't come straight out the top of the unit; they pop in and push down. However, I found that it could easily fit on the other side of the drive bays if I cut a hole in the side cover. I figured it would look cool that way, too.

Atari 2600

The Atari was the easiest component to add. I had a junior model, so it didn't even have to be taken apart (except for rewiring the switches). It would mount behind the PC motherboard with the power supplies.

Tools and Supplies

As with most projects, this one required the use of many tools and supplies. Here is a list of the ones I used:

- Soldering iron (adjustable power supply)
- Rosin core solder
- Heat-shrink tubing (various sizes)
- Electrical tape
- Cordless drill (doesn't need to be cordless)
- Torqx drivers
- Phillips screwdrivers (No. 1 and No. 2)
- Flathead screwdriver (No. 2)
- Utility knife
- X-acto knife
- Tweezers
- Wire strippers
- Paint (yellow, red, white)
- Dremel tool

- Rotary cutter
- Jigsaw
- Goggles
- Soda (with lots of caffeine)
- Chips
- Coffee, coffee, and more coffee

And here is a list of the major components I used:

- Lian-Li PC-76 case
- Microsoft Xbox
- Sony PlayStation 2
- Nintendo GameCube and an 8-bit Nintendo
- Atari 2600 Jr.
- Epox 8K3A+ mobo
- AMD XP 2100+ CPU
- ATI Radeon All-In-Wonder 8500DV video card
- Kingston PC2700 333MHz DDR RAM 512MB
- Intel Pro/100 NIC
- Six-position 9-pin switch box
- 14 various toggle switches
- TDK 16/10/40 CD-RW drive
- Seagate 40GB HD
- Thermaltake Volcano 7+ CPU heat sink; also Thermaltake active and passive memory coolers
- Various bolts, nuts, zip ties, heat-shrink tubing, plastic sheeting, and other hardware

Putting Yoshi's Boxx Together

Now it's time to start cutting and soldering. You know, the fun part—power toys...er, I mean tools.

1. Cut out the top of the case for the GameCube. I carefully measured the GameCube and marked the top of the case with tape, as shown in Figure 6.3. Remember that when the lid opens, you need extra room for the lid to clear the case.

> **Remember to wear eye protection, and try to get someone to help you.**

6.3 Masking off the area where the cutout for the GameCube will be.

I used a cut-off wheel on the Dremel and carefully followed the masked lines. Once the straight lines were done, I drilled the corners to finish the cut, and then used a file to clean up the sides and corners.

2. Cut out a hole for the power outlet. This should be in the rear of the machine because other cords will be attached here as well, and the power supplies are central to the rear of the machine.

3. Cut out a hole for the AV plugs. I placed this in the rear of the machine close to the other connectors so it would look as if it was supposed to be there. See Figure 6.4.

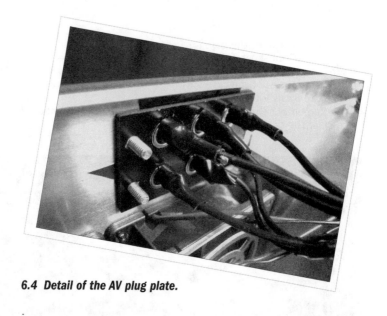

6.4 Detail of the AV plug plate.

4. Cut holes for the GameCube controllers in a blank 5.25-inch drive bay cover. I used the stock cover from the GameCube as a template to mark the blank drive bay cover. I then drilled a pilot hole and used the Dremel to enlarge the holes so that they would be exactly the size of the controller ports. See Figure 6.5.

6.5 GameCube controller ports and the drive bay cover that I modified to accept them.

5. Cut holes for the Xbox controllers in a blank 5.25-inch drive bay cover. Both sets of controller ports were originally glued together so I could use them as a template to cut out the opening. After the opening was cut out and shaped with a file, I drilled the mounting hole through the controller port block and the bay cover for the mounting screws. See Figure 6.6.

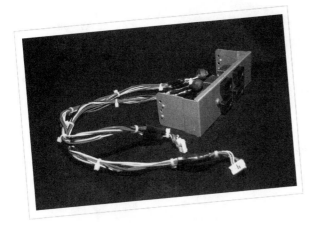

6.6 The Xbox controller ports mounted in the drive bay cover.

6. Cut a hole for the Xbox DVD in a blank 5.25-inch drive bay cover. This was measured and cut out without a template. It is a straightforward layout, and the face of the tray overlaps, covering up any variation in the opening. See Figure 6.7.

6.7 Xbox DVD drive with modified drive bay cover glued in place.

7. Cut holes for the Xbox Power and Eject buttons in the front cover of the Boxx case. I chose to mount them next to the main PC Power buttons. I also aligned them to maintain the pleasing visual layout.

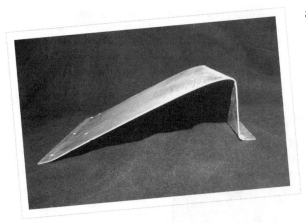

8. Make a mounting plate for the Xbox mobo, as shown in Figure 6.8. The Xbox mobo and the PC mobo will be mounted side by side. The AV connector needs to clear the PC mobo, so I used a raised mounting plate.

6.8 The aluminum plate I made to mount the Xbox motherboard onto, inside the case.

9. Drill holes for the mounting plate and power supply. I laid the mounting base on the plate in the case and marked the holes, then drilled them outside of the case.

10. Cut out the front panel for the PlayStation 2. Make sure your measurement is accurate because this is the most visible part of the Boxx, and it can't be undone. See Figure 6.9.

6.9 The PlayStation 2 mounted on the front panel.

11. Cut out the side panels for the Nintendo, the Atari, and the window, as shown in Figure 6.10. Again, measure carefully and multiple times. Remember the old saying: "Measure twice, cut once."

Cutouts for Nintendo, Atari, and side window

6.10 Side panels for the Nintendo, the Atari, and the window.

Mod the Xbox

1. Cut out the base of the Xbox for the mobo mount, as shown in Figure 6.11.

2. Cut out the base for the power supply mount.

6.11 Cutout Xbox case bottom, which is used to mount the Xbox motherboard onto the aluminum plate.

3. Cut extra material off the DVD drive.

4. Extend the wiring for the game controller ports, DVD connector, Power/Eject buttons, and hard-drive power, as shown in Figure 6.12.

6.12 The controller port wires have been spliced to make them longer.

5. Glue two Xbox controller ports together and mount them in the 5.25-inch cover. See Figure 6.13.

6. Glue the 5.25-inch cover to the DVD drive.

6.13 Shown from the back, the ports are glued together.

7. Solder the AV wire onto the breakout panel, as shown in Figure 6.14.

8. Solder the power supply power lead.

6.14 *The AV wire soldered to the breakout panel.*

Mod the GameCube

1. Solder the power supply lead.

2. Mount the controller in the 5.25-inch cover after the GameCube is installed in the case (space constraint).

3. Sand the thickness of the GameCube case. This may seem obvious, but remove all components from the case before sanding. See Figure 6.15.

6.15 *GameCube after the case has been sanded with a belt sander to enable it to fit into the drive bay.*

Mod the PlayStation 2

1. Solder the power and eject switch leads.
2. Make the mounting bracket.
3. Cut out the front face of the PlayStation 2 for use on the front case panel.

Mod the 8-bit Nintendo

1. Open the Nintendo box and use the standard mounting posts for mounting it in the new case.
2. Carefully measure the required height and cut the posts accordingly.
3. Use epoxy, marine glue, or some other kind of high-strength adhesive to glue the posts in position on the sides of the drive bay. Be sure to leave enough access space so you can move drives in and out of the bays.

Mod the Atari

Not many changes are needed for the Atari. Just rewire the reset and select switches.

Power Supplies

Because I had a few power supplies, I figured it would look cool to open them up so I could see all their parts. I used a marine adhesive to glue them in place next to the Atari. But be careful to insulate them from transmitting power to the chassis. You don't want to create a dangerous hazard.

Once you have all the components installed, there are a couple of details to address. An obvious detail is cable management. Take the time to go through all the wiring to make it look neat and tidy. Use cable wrap or sleeving to bundle wires together to give them a slimmer, more orderly look. Run some tests to make sure that everything is working.

If everything is working, invite your friends over and get your game on!

Y-Boxx 2K3: The Revision

The first Yoshi's Boxx was about fitting as many consoles into one unit as I could. The new Boxx, the Y-Boxx 2K3, is about fitting the components I really want into one unit.

When planning the new Boxx, I looked at the original, saw what I wanted to keep, and then decided what should be added. See Figure 6.16.

6.16 Y-Boxx 2K3.

Here's what's in the Y-Boxx:

- Microsoft Xbox
- Sony PlayStation 2
- Nintendo GameCube
- Windows PC
    - 3.06-GHz Pentium 4 CPU
    - MSI GNB Max motherboard
    - Zalman CNPS7000-Cu heat sink

- NVIDIA GeForce FX
- Toshiba slot-loading DVD drive
- Klipsch ProMedia GMX D5.1 speakers
- Audio Authority 1154 component video automatic selector
- Buffalo Technology AirStation
- NEC MT1060 projector
- A whole lot of plastic, aluminum, rivets, screws, and more

Building Y-Boxx 2K3

My first problem with this project: wires. The wires for the controllers, Ethernet, power, video, and audio can create a tangled mess that's out of control. So, I decided to go wireless with just a single wire for power. Going wireless was a lot easier than I thought it would be. The game consoles have wireless controllers, so that was convenient. I then used an 802.11 bridge to connect the PC and consoles to the Internet.

Built-In AV

Another big difference between the original Boxx and the new one is the integration of audio and video. After much thought, I finally decided on using a projector for video. A built-in screen has a fixed screen size, and I wanted the option of playing on a 50-foot screen. Who wouldn't?

When it came to the Boxx's audio components, I toyed with adding a 150-watts-per-channel amp, but it would have been too big and much too expensive. Instead, I went with a Klipsch Promedia GMX D5.1 system, as shown in Figure 6.17. It's affordable, it sounds great, and it's the size I wanted.

6.17 Y-Boxx with the Klipsch Promedia GMX D5.1 system installed.

Use a Drink Coaster, Please

Once I decided on the components I wanted to use, I started thinking about how they would all fit together in the new Boxx. Obviously, the Boxx had to be bigger than the original one. Keeping size in mind, I decided to turn the Boxx into a coffee table. This works well because the Boxx should sit between the screen and me if the speakers are to sound right. See Figure 6.18.

6.18 Detail showing speaker and air vent cutouts.

I played with different shapes for the Boxx. But after mulling over an abstract design, I settled on the classic cube. Building the Boxx wasn't hard. It was a matter of careful measurements and checking all cuts two or three times before making them.

My trusty laser cutter from Universal Laser Systems made cutting the plastic much cleaner and easier. But laser cutters demand accurate measurements because the laser does exactly what you tell it to do, even if you tell it to do the wrong thing.

Now that the new Boxx is finished, I can finally get some sleep. However, I already have some new ideas to upgrade my Y-Boxx. (I'll save the upgrade for a later project.) I still have a few details to clean up, but it won't stop me from enjoying many, many hours of supersize gaming mayhem.

Chapter 7

Quirky and Cool

Whether you want to make your case stealth quiet, find a use for that old ammo can, submerge your expensive components in liquid, or just give up and let the ants take over, there is but one reason. Because we can.

Project YS-2: Building a Silent Computer Case

I often find myself thinking, "Gee, I want a loud computer, one so loud I can't concentrate on anything else!" The tinnitus will drown out the noise anyway. I'm sure you've thought the same. Well, of course you haven't. We all hate loud machines, and unless you are in a server room, there is no need to have an insanely loud computer.

What I do find is that I like to use my computer as a home theatre and music source, and my overclocked, highly cooled rig just doesn't serve this function well. After giving it a great deal of thought, I realized that there is no reason I can't have a good gaming rig that is perfectly silent. With the ever-growing segment of computer consumers wanting their systems to run as quietly as possible, more and more companies are focusing their attention on making products that run just as well but are also quiet. Manufacturers are now making components that range from silent CPU coolers to ultra-quiet drives and case fans.

To start the project, choose your hardware with care. Here is a list of components and supplies I used, and you might want to use them too:

- Zalman CNPS 7000-Cu
- Zalman ZM80A-HP VGA cooler
- Vantec's VAN520A Stealth power supply
- Vantec's Stealth fans (120mm and 80mm)
- Seagate Barracuda Serial ATA V hard drive
- Sony DRU500AX DVD burner
- Lian-Li PC6070
- Dynamat
- PAX Mate
- Melamine

Let's begin with the CPU cooler. The Zalman CNPS 7000-Cu (`www.zalmanusa.com`) is shown in Figure 7.1.

It's a good idea to use air cooling for this application because it is easy to work with and will not intrude on valuable space inside the case that you'll need to muffle other components. This cooler is so quiet that you can barely hear it running, even without a case cover in place.

7.1 CPU heat sink installed.

The Zalman ZM80A-HP VGA cooler works by using two large surface area heat sinks that are linked together by a heat pipe around the video card. There is no fan so it is completely silent. To test it, I left it running in a system for 48 hours straight, looping Futuremark's 3Dmark 03 Pro the entire time. It got very warm to the touch but did not fail or reach unstable temperatures.

Vantec's VAN520A Stealth power supply (`http://vantecusa.com/`) fits nicely into the case. It is very quiet out of the box, but if you want it even quieter, mod it a little. You can rewire the two inlet fans within it to control themselves using the fan's speed controller. This allows you to adjust the speed of the fans down to a level that is still acceptable for airflow but much quieter. You can also use some of Vantec's Stealth fans, which come in various sizes.

In this project, I found it best to use the 120mm for inlet air and the 80mm for outlet. It is important that you have a balance of air in and out of the case. There are other options available for quiet fans such as Panaflo or NMB.

Check out http://store.yahoo.com/xoxide/12vastfan.html and http://store.yahoo.com/xoxide/80vanstealfa.html for more details about the fans mentioned.

Seagate has been making some very quiet drives for a while, so the Seagate Barracuda Serial ATA V is a good hard drive to use. It does not disappoint. As is usual for this line of drives, it is very quiet.

Choosing a DVD drive is difficult. Be sure to listen to each of your options before purchasing one. I listened to many drives, and all of them had a good amount of noise when running. You might have to resign yourself to the fact that you will have to add a lot of extra sound insulation around the drive. Another solution is to break down and buy a DVD burner if you can. My choice is the Sony DRU500AX.

Once you get it home, be sure to test whether it is reading properly. I tested mine with a DVD, and to my delight, it was perfectly silent while playing DVDs. Unfortunately, after checking it by installing a few programs, I found that it was noisy while spinning up a CD-ROM, but once it was up to speed, it was very quiet. For those who can't afford a DVD burner, try the Toshiba SD-M1712 DVD drive.

Sound Through the Case

Usually, sound waves hit the case panels and force them to move. As they move, the panels push the air on the other side, causing the transmitted sound, which is how a speaker cone works. Other noises can be heard through openings in the case as well. To reduce these sounds, you need to focus on two factors: increasing the density or stiffness of the panels and dissipating the sound waves. Cellular or fibrous materials dissipate sound, with a greater thickness absorbing lower frequencies; whereas heavy, limp materials decrease resonance, reducing higher frequencies.

A number of materials can be used for this type of application. In my project, I started with a Lian-Li PC6070, courtesy of Xoxide.com (see Figure 7.2). It comes with a layer of foam preinstalled on the inside top, front cover, and side covers. It is a nice solid case. The front door panel is thick as well, so it helps reduce transmitted noise.

But of course, you want to make sure this project is "stealth" silent. So try taking off the foam that comes with the case and putting in your own mix of silencing materials.

I recommend starting with a layer of Dynamat, then a layer of PAX Mate, and then finishing it off with as many layers of Melamine foam as you can fit into the case. See Figure 7.3.

7.2 PC6070 case after painting and laser etching.

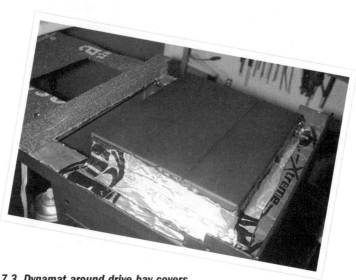

7.3 Dynamat around drive bay covers.

The Dynamat works through what is called *Vibro-Acoustic Energy Conversion*. Basically, it takes the sound energy (vibrations in the case) and converts it to low-grade thermal energy.

PAX Mate are foam mats that reduce vibrations and dissipate noise.

The Melamine dissipates the sound even further. If you're not able to use as thick a layer as you would like, just put in as much as you can fit.

Sound from Case Fan Air Passages

The case fans and gaps in the case also allow sounds to escape. The best way to reduce these sounds is to construct a series of sound barriers for them to go through. The principle I adhere to is to use stiff dividing partitions coupled with good sound dissipating materials as shown in Figure 7.4. Most of the sounds that would have escaped through the fan areas are then muffled below what can be heard.

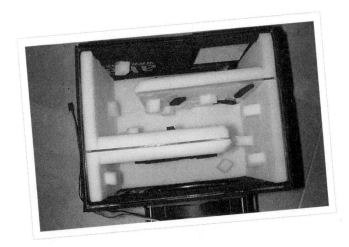

7.4 Inlet air box with side removed.

Of course heat is still an issue, and you want a proper amount of air transfer within the case, so make sure that airflow is not adversely affected. For the inlet, I built an air box to dampen the noise. It makes the air go through a series of passages that have been treated to reduce noise. For the rear, I made a simple single stage baffle to diffuse sound from the air outlets.

To cut out the complex parts for the air baffles, I used a Universal Laser Systems laser cutter. This made it very easy to cut pieces and etch the designs in the panels.

To measure the sound coming from the case at this point, you can perform a couple of tests.

Sound is measured in a few different ways. A-weighted decibels and C-weighted decibels and Flat are all averages of the entire spectrum. When you see figures posted for sound level, most of the time you will see them in A-weighted specs. This is considered to be the average range that humans hear and more precisely the range in which hearing can be damaged. The weighting of a sound meter basically adjusts the reading to compensate for these frequencies. Table 7.1 contains information about how a weighting system works.

Table 7.1
How a Weighting System Works

Frequency (Hz)	Curve A (dB)	Curve C (dB)
16	-56.7	-8.5
31.5	-39.4	-3
63	-26.2	-0.8
125	-16.1	-0.2
250	-8.6	0
500	-3.2	0
1000	0	0
2000	1.2	-0.2
4000	1.0	-0.8
8000	-1.1	-3
16000	-6.6	-8.5

When I tested the sound coming from my case, I was getting Sound Pressure Level (SPL) that was below the room level. I realized I needed to use the 1/3 octave Real Time Analyzer (RTA) mode and a very quiet room. Unfortunately, I was unable to get an accurate reading in the rooms I had available to me, so I contacted the folks over at Dolby Labs, and they agreed to let me use one of their quiet rooms, which had a room tone that was giving me a 0~5db reading. To perform the test, I used a Larson-Davis 824 sound level meter. The meter controls were very easy to figure out once I understood the readings and numbers I was looking at. Table 7.2 contains the test results along with some comparison measurements.

Table 7.2
Test Results

Component	Level
Stock OEM PC	38db
Laptop (with fan on)	42db
Project YS-2	8db (120 hz and above); 14db (100 hz and below)

Okay, here is the disclaimer. Because the difference between the room level and the box is so small, the accuracy of the reading is questionable. From a subjective standpoint, the YS-2 was completely silent from three feet away.

Just to give you an idea of various noises and the decibel levels they produce, Table 7.3 provides a listing of common sounds and their levels.

I would like to thank Xoxide.com, Dynamat, Vantec, Larson-Davis, Seagate, Toshiba, soundsuckers.com, and Universal Laser Systems for their assistance on this project.

Table 7.3
Decibel Levels for Common Events

Typical Noises	Levels
Rocket launching	180db
Jet taking off	140db
Air raid siren	125db
Threshold of pain	120db
Loud rock music	115db
Ear damage starts	85db
Busy street	70db
Normal conversation	60db
Yoshi's cubicle	46db
Library	40db
Rustling leaves	30db
Yoshi's movie room	24db
Soft whisper	20db
Threshold of sound perception	10db
Threshold of human hearing	0db

Project: Build a Submersion Cooling Case

We've tried all kinds of methods to keep our computers cool. Probably the most unique method we've tried is to submerge the motherboard and processor in liquid. As you know, liquid and electricity don't mix, so we couldn't just use plain water. Instead, we used hydrofluoroether from 3M—specifically, HFE-7100.

HFE-7100 is a dielectric fluid used in thermal management applications. Translation: It does not conduct any electricity, won't harm electronic components, and is an excellent conductor of heat. The downside to HFE-7100 is that it's expensive (about $220 per gallon), and it will evaporate very quickly if not sealed, which means we need to construct the appropriate containment system.

Many ways can be used to construct a case and cooling system for this application. We used a clear acrylic case, mostly for aesthetics. You can also use something as simple as a Styrofoam cooler, which is an excellent insulator and allows you to use liquid nitrogen to cool the HFE. Figure 7.5 shows the finished submersion cooling system.

7.5 Finished submersion cooling system.

First, let's look at the parts you'll need:

- One 17-inch (length) by 30-inch (width) by 1/4-inch (thickness) clear acrylic panel
- Two 7-inch by 30-inch by 1/4-inch clear acrylic panels
- Four 7-inch by 16.5-inch by 1/4-inch clear acrylic panels
- Two 17-inch by 15-inch by 1/4-inch clear acrylic panels
- Liquid acrylic cement
- Silicon sealant
- Masking tape
- 1/4-inch copper refrigerant tubing
- Pipe-bending tool
- Magnetic drive fountain pump
- 90-degree 3/4-inch NPT fitting

- 3/4-inch NPT to 1/2-inch barb fitting
- 1/2-inch braided tubing
- Two 1-inch stainless steel hose clamps
- Four gallons HFE-7100
- 40 pounds of dry ice

Construction of the case is quite simple. Draw out what you want to build, then carefully calculate your dimensions, taking into account the thickness of your materials.

Now, let's put the case together.

Construct the Case

Before you get started, make sure you practice good safety habits. Always wear goggles to protect your eyes while you build the case and while handling the HFE. You should wear rubber gloves to protect your hands as well. Although studies have shown that HFE is nontoxic and safe when it comes in contact with the skin, it is still very cold. There's no good reason not to take these precautions.

Construction is straightforward. Here are the steps:

1. Bend the copper tubing to create a cooler, as shown in Figure 7.6.
2. Cut out the holes for the cooler to go through the panels.

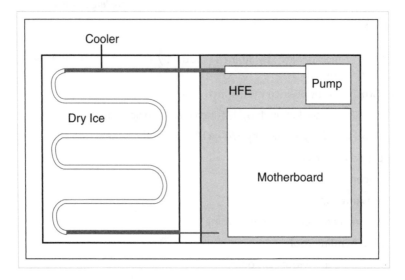

7.6 Diagram of planned submersion cooling system.

3. Use masking tape to hold the sides and panels in place.

4. Insert the cooler at this point because it will be very difficult to put it in after the panels are in place. Use the liquid acrylic cement to glue the panels together.

5. After the sides and panels are glued into place, use the silicon sealant to seal all joints and to seal the cooler to the two panels.

6. Cut out a relief in the side for the pump power, IDE, PS/2, and VGA cables to come through.

7. After the wires and cables are in place, seal them with silicon sealant.

8. Test your configuration with water and no other electronic components except for the pump in place. Tape the cables up to keep them from getting in the water. Look for leaks or any problems.

9. Place the motherboard in the box and connect the cables.

10. Pour in the HFE-7100.

11. Put the dry ice in the cooling side and start the pump. Let it run for 10 minutes before you start the computer. It will take time to cool the HFE-7100, and it is important that you cool the HFE-7100 before starting the computer.

Project: YM-23, Ammo Can PC

I have been toying with the idea of putting together an ammo can PC for a while now. But first I had a couple of details to iron out. For example, what would I use the PC for, and how big would I want it to be? Initially, I wanted it to be a hard-core gaming rig. But after taking the small size of the ammo can into consideration I realized it just wouldn't work. If I wanted a full-size rig, I might as well use one of my more flashy cases. What I was shooting for was something that looked cool and was very portable. So, because I wasn't going for the gaming end, I decided to make it a portable file server. It would be perfect for MP3 swapping parties.

Once my project had a goal, the next step was to decide on the components to use. Here is a list of the components I chose:

- Epia motherboard
- Lynksys WMP54G 802.11G PCI card
- Sparkle micro ATX power supply
- Western Digital 120GB special edition hard drive
- 7.62mm 200-round surplus ammunition case

Choosing the Epia mobo was easy. I wanted to use the smallest components possible, and I happened to have one in my workshop, which meant no additional outlay of cashola.

The Sparkle power supply was hard to find. I finally found one in stock at a little hole in the wall store in my neighborhood. The hard drive was also lying around in my workshop. I truly believe in using what I have on hand rather than spending more money for no good reason. The ammo case was the smallest case I could find that still fit all the components I wanted to include. Notice that I chose not to install a CD-ROM drive. Obviously, space was my main consideration. Once the operating system was loaded, if I really needed to install a program, I figured I could always do it from a network drive or use an external USB drive.

How I Made It

I made plastic mounting plates for the mobo and power supply. To get everything to fit, I had to take apart the power supply. Precious millimeters make a difference. To make the mounting plates I used my trusty laser cutter.

Once the mounts were made, I used them as a template to drill the holes in the ammo can. I then cut out the holes for the mobo in/outs. I used the bracket that comes with the mobo as a template to mark the ammo can as shown in Figure 7.7.

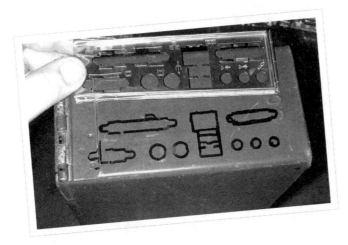

7.7 Template and planned cuts on the side of the ammo box.

To cut it out, I used a Dremel with a fiber cut-off disc. It cut through the metal can like butter and made quick work of the job as shown in Figure 7.8. To clean up the edges, I used a small metal file.

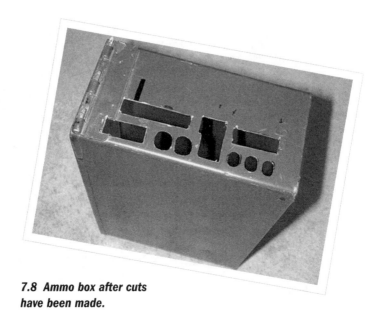

7.8 Ammo box after cuts have been made.

Once I had the mobo, hard drive, and power supply mounted, I realized that I had enough space to add an 802.11 card. See Figure 7.9.

7.9 All components installed including the 802.11 card.

The card made it look real cool with the antenna sticking out the back—just like a military radio. See Figure 7.10.

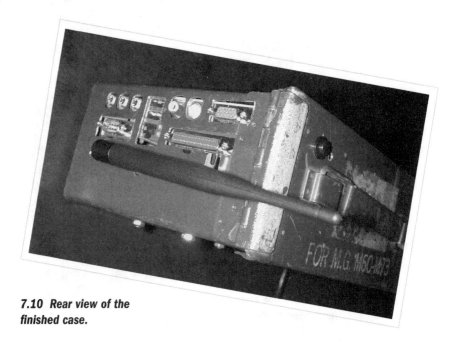

7.10 Rear view of the finished case.

Once all the mounting holes were completed, it was time to put it all together and make sure it worked. See Figure 7.11.

Success!

7.11 It looks cool and it works!

Give Your PC the Creepy Crawlies

By Kevin Rose

I've been racking my brain trying to figure out a case mod that will shock the mod community. I finally gave up and resorted to my backup plan: I decided to put an ant farm in my PC case.

Huh? Did you say *ant farm*?

I did. Where did I get this idea? I have no idea. I've loved ant farms since I was a young lad. I thought this would be a great opportunity to bring them back into the popular culture, but with a digital twist.

Ants don't eat a whole lot and don't mind hot temperatures. They're perfect for my XP 2200+ PC.

Here's what I used to put my ant farm PC together:

- One Uncle Milton's Giant Ant Farm.
- One window cut into my PC case. Yoshi has some great instructions on how to cut a case window. You can also use a case with a precut window.
- One large piece of 1/8-inch clear plastic. I got mine at the local TAP Plastics.
- One saw to cut the plastic.
- Nontoxic adhesive.

Constructing the farm was easy. I simply duplicated the layout of the farm inside the window of the computer case. Once I had duplicated the layout, I cut the plastic to match. Then I used the glue to attach the farm to the window.

Chapter 8

Spotlight on Mods

The modding community is huge and growing every day. Still, it's pretty tight-knit, and these artists never get as much credit as they deserve. That's why I decided to dedicate a chapter of my book to some of the mods that intrigued me. I chose these mods because each one appealed to me in a different way. Unfortunately, space in the book limited me to just a sampling of the wonderful mods out there. Because I'm a total gearhead, the AMD Big Block was an obvious choice. And because I love cheesy sci-fi flicks, I was immediately drawn to the Biohazard mod.

Although I'm a technology junky, I also appreciate styles from the past. That's why I chose to feature mods built inside antiques, like Technotone and ToAsTOr. Some of the projects make me nostalgic for more personal reasons. I've never lost that child-hood fascination with military gear, so when I saw the PC made out of a bomb assembly, it just grabbed me. Both of my grandfathers were woodworkers, my father is a woodworker, and I do some woodworking as well. The wood case reminded me of projects I used to do with my dad.

The following stories are in no particular order. I appreciate all the mods and their respective modders equally.

Here is a list of the mods showcased in this chapter:

- Homemade Steel and Glass PC Case by Keith Nolen
- Surface to Surface PC by Chris Adams
- Technotone by Gareth Powell
- The Mg3 NeXT Cube by Barry Collins, a.k.a Cold Dog
- The Humidor Series by Jeffrey L. Stephenson
- AMD Big Block by Rainer Wingende a.k.a heaDrOOMx
- The ToAsTOr by Joe Klingler
- Biohazard by Paul Capello, a.k.a Crimson Sky
- Hemophilia by Jerami Campbell
- The Mailbox Mod by Jeff Neima
- Wood Case by Mikko Syrjälä
- The Tech Tube by Troy "T-Bone" Ervin
- The LokiCube by Tino Stephan

Homemade Steel and Glass PC Case

Keith Nolen is a firefighter from Beaumont, Texas. He's married and has an 8-year-old daughter who likes SpongeBob SquarePants. He enjoys woodworking and customizing, and recently sacrificed a quarter inch off the top of his thumb on the sacred alter of the mod.

Keith became involved in the craft of modding by way of overclocking. While learning how to speed up his system three or four years ago, he came across a web site featuring pictures of a modded case. It was just a box with a window and a neon light inside, but he had to try the same thing himself. He decided to put a simple window in his big, old Aopen case, and he's been hooked ever since.

Keith's magnum opus is the Homemade Steel and Glass Case shown in Figure 8.1. It's 21-inches tall, 21-inches deep, and 9-inches wide. The glass on the sides and bottom is 1/8-inch thick, and according to Keith, was "a real humdinger to work with." The steel wasn't any kinder. On his web site (`http://home.cmaaccess.com/~knolen`) Keith warns, "steel elongates quite a bit when heated and burns flesh instantly when you least expect it."

8.1 Keith's Homemade Steel and Glass Case.

For this project, Keith used the following supplies:

- 3/4-inch square steel tubing
- 1/2-inch square steel tubing
- 1/8-inch thick glass
- Plexiglas
- Silver solder
- Clear fans
- Silver rounded cables
- Mirrored glass bottom
- Red cold cathode light
- 20 feet of EL wire
- Raidmax power supply
- Glass gems for power and reset buttons
- Skull domed case sticker
- Laser blue and green LEDs

Like others of his modding ilk, Keith asserts that part of his drive to complete any project comes from people who tell him it can't be done. Regarding the Homemade Steel and Glass Case he says, "My buddies told me I was nuts for starting a project like this, and I hate to prove them wrong."

The name of Keith's case doesn't necessarily do it justice. He used steel tubing, glass, and Plexiglas, but he also used good quality silver solder, glass gems for his Power and Reset buttons, a red cold cathode light, and pearl white paint meant for a 2002 Cadillac. He admits, however, that the paint was a waste of money because its true shine can only be appreciated in the sunlight.

Keith maintains that the parts were pretty simple and straightforward, but his cache of tools were another story. He had to use a miter saw with a metal cutting blade to cut the metal. "It worked great," he says, "except for the barrage of sparks that constantly threatened to set my head or arm hair on fire." He also used a MAPP gas torch to solder the metal and a grinding wheel to clean it up. Keith did nearly all the work himself except for the sandblasting to remove the rust, which he left to the professionals. Keith disdained professional glass drilling, however, because of the high prices. "They even said I would get charged for the pieces they broke," he laughs. Instead he used a drill press and a diamond-coated drill bit. "With some antifreeze for a lubricant, you can drill one hole about every five minutes," he says. "Slow is good when you're drilling glass."

In total, the case cost $300, but Keith said it could be made for less. He blames the increase in price on the braze welding. "To braze weld strong joints, you have to use the good silver solder and it's pricey."

It took Keith six months to finish the case. Keith actually made two frames in the event that he irreversibly messed up one in the process. "Some days I was a driven lunatic and got a lot accomplished," he recalls, "but then there were the other days…days when I would just stare at the stupid thing wondering what I needed to do next or trying to figure out where it all went so wrong."

He can't remember how many late nights were involved, but he admits, "My poor kidneys will remember the Mountain Dew from this project for years to come." Still, Keith says his only regrets are that he didn't include a way to hide all the wires and that he didn't chrome the frame. The latter mod would have cost several hundred dollars, so he chose not to.

Right now Keith uses the Steel and Glass case as his primary system, but he's working on a new mod called Stormbringer (named after the fantasy book by Michael Moorcock). So far, Stormbringer has cost Keith a 1/4 inch off the top of one of his thumbs, but according to the pictures of the case he has posted in the GruntvillE forums (www.gruntville.com), it looks like it might be worth it. After all, he has another thumb.

Surface to Surface PC

As a child, Chris Adams used to take apart his toys and put them back together again, creating something entirely different. "I guess I still do," he says, "I get bored easily."

His major mod project is called KiSA, Surface to Surface PC, which is shown in Figure 8.2. KiSA is an acronym for a nickname Chris was given while he was in the Air Force: King Smart Ass. The term "Surface to Surface" comes from the fact that he created the mod from part of a disarmed bomb.

8.2 Chris's KiSA, Surface to Surface PC.

For this project, Chris used the following supplies:

- U.S. Air Force surplus Mk 81, Low Drag General Purpose (LDGP) bomb tail assembly
- Band aids
- Rounded cables
- Plexiglas
- Rough aluminum
- A piano hinge
- Paint
- Stainless steel mixing bowl for the nosecone
- 80mm Antec LED fans
- 120mm motherboard cooling fan
- Power supply unit (PSU) fan
- CPU fan

The KiSA project started when Chris came across two bona fide U.S. Air Force surplus Mk 81, Low Drag General Purpose (LDGP) bomb tail assemblies. He gave one to a friend and kept one for himself. Chris's assembly is now an 800 MHz PC running Linux Red Hat 8 and his friend's assembly is an ashtray.

Before the military disposed of the tail assembly, it crushed the assembly in two different places so it could no longer be used for its original purpose. Thus, the only mass destruction this weapon ever caused is the battery of metal splinters Chris received during the construction of the mod. With the help of a friend, a hydraulic press, and a torch, Chris managed to repair one of the dents in the tail and get it looking almost new again.

The first step in creating the bomb mod was to create two windows in the body of the tail section, one for the fan and one for the video cables to pass through. Chris then covered the windows with Plexiglas, which he says bends easily when it's heated to 170 degrees. Because Chris only had possession of the tail of the bomb, he had to create the body. For this he used an old PC tower. "I ran it through a metal bender a few dozen times until it came out the nice cylindrical shape that you now see."

To access the drives, Chris created a bay door and added a piano hinge to the upper half of the case. The parts were so snug inside that he had to use rounded IDE cables so the drive connections wouldn't interfere with the closing mechanism of the door.

The pièce de résistance is the creatively Dremeled, drilled, and riveted stainless steel mixing bowl that serves as the nosecone of the KiSA. The grill cover is a laser cut acrylic guard sporting the image of Tux, the loveable Linux mascot. It's lit from the back by an 80mm Antec red LED fan, as shown in Figure 8.3.

8.3 KiSA's grill cover lit by a red LED fan.

Chris finished the Surface to Surface PC in January 2003 "due to prompting from my wife to get it done for *Maximum PC*'s patriotic PC contest," he says. Chris didn't win the contest, but his mod did appear in the magazine.

In total, the project took about three weeks, four bags of coffee beans, and $400. His biggest challenge, Chris recounts, was working in such a small space. The entire mod is only 42 inches long and 7.75 inches in diameter. And, he says, "I have big hands." For the motherboard, he started with a Shuttle FV24, but it had a few problems, so he ended up using the tiny VIA EPIA, which measures just 170mm × 170mm. More information about the mod can found at `http://kisa_444.tripod.com`.

Chris offers some advice for anyone attempting his own mod. "Research all facets of design and application," he warns. The first time he turned on the PC for a test run, he blew out the power supply because the video card that was connected to the motherboard and a metal-plated On/Off switch grounded the whole thing out.

KiSA is Chris's first major mod unless you count his tattoos. Figures 8.4 and 8.5 show the final product.

Currently, he's working on putting a Flex ATX board into a pay phone. If he had unlimited money, time, and resources he says, right now he'd be working on a sort of high-tech La-Z-Boy, or as he describes it, "a computer recliner with split keyboards, half per arm, Panasonic Virtual Reality glasses simulating a 60-inch screen, and all the other components built neatly into the base." To that end, he is currently in search of corporate sponsorship and says, "If Bill Gates or Dean Kamen are reading this, then send some of your loot this way."

8.4 Close-up of KiSA, side view.

8.5 Full view of KiSA.

Technotone

Any modder worth his weight in solder knows that a hot spot on the web for case mods is www.pheaton.com. The site not only offers tutorials and modding news, but also forums where members can create their own work logs, post pictures, and receive feedback as they create their works of art. It's a unique and highly supportive community for expert modders and newbies alike.

The man behind Pheaton, Gareth "Lord Pheaton" Powell, champions the work of modders from all over the world, but he's also something of a talent himself. One of his masterpieces is a case built out of an old console radio. He calls it Technotone, which is shown in Figure 8.6.

8.6 Technotone.

For this project, Gareth used the following supplies:

- Retro console radio shell
- 40 feet of 1/4-inch angled aluminum
- 10 feet of drive chain
- 4 sprockets
- Windshield-wiper motor from a Saturn
- Custom-made micro switches
- 4 square feet of diamond plate aluminum
- 10-inch flaming speaker grill
- 2 slide bearings (for the removable motherboard tray)
- Old 250 watt AT power supply (for the lift)
- Accenting fabric
- Chrome-look door trim
- Velcro
- Rivets
- Screws

Hardware used included the following:

- Intel P4 2.4 GHz
- Intel 845I motherboard
- 512MB Rambus
- NVIDIA GeForce4 Ti 4600
- 60GB hard drive
- 15-inch Sony LCD monitor
- Matrix Orbital VK204 VFD character display

Although Technotone is one of the most creative custom cases, Gareth's modding career started not out of artistic expression but out of frustration. His PC was running so hot that even a huge heat sink wouldn't keep the system from shutting down when he was gaming. "So, I busted out a rotary tool and cut an 80mm blowhole on the top of the case," Gareth says. Thus, a modder was born.

Gareth is currently working on his fantasy mod. He already has it completely designed and is now seeking the whopping $70,000 it will take to make it a reality. All he'll say about the secret project is that it will "revolutionize the way people think about case modding."

His new mod may be forward-looking, but Technotone is a fitting tribute to the past. And with it, Gareth continues his history of practical modding. He admits that Technotone was an experimental design he came up with when his neighbor decided to get rid of his old console radio. But this mod wasn't just built on a whim; it has a definite practical side. Gareth explains, "I wanted to make a system that would be functional, yet fit with the décor of the home." Not only did he build this mod inside a tasteful piece of furniture, but he also managed to get rid of all those ugly wires. Technotone is equipped with 802.11b connectivity plus a wireless keyboard and mouse.

The final stunning touch is the retractable 15-inch Sony LCD monitor. Gareth included custom-made circuitry and micro switches for one-touch operation, which allows the monitor to disappear from view. "The concept was to blend the system into the aged construction of the radio," says Gareth, "so when it was not in use, the computer would be unobtrusive."

Gareth built Technotone to take to the Cyberathlete Professional League (CPL) competition, which he attends every six months. It took fourth place in the CPL C3* Contest in the summer of 2002. The PC has since been "decommissioned," and Gareth says it "sits in my hallway begging for attention, like the four other systems in my home."

Inside this 1950s era radio, Gareth has managed to hide about 40 feet of 1/4-inch angled aluminum, 10 feet of drive chain, 4 sprockets, 4 square feet of diamond plate aluminum, 2 slide bearings for the removable motherboard tray, an old 250 watt AT power supply (for the lift), and a windshield-wiper motor from an old Saturn. It also packs a punch with an Intel P4 2.4 GHz and a 60GB hard drive.

Technotone is about 36-inches tall, 30-inches wide, and weighs about 75 pounds fully assembled. Gareth estimates that with the hardware, monitor, gears, motors, raw metal, and additional accessories, Technotone cost him around $3000 to create. This figure also includes all the experimentation that went into the project. It took three months to build, and he adds, "roughly two months of hard labor and late nights." On the positive side, Gareth says, "I managed to escape with nothing more than a few skinned knuckles and one minor electrocution." And, of course, one beautiful mod. See Figures 8.7 and 8.8.

8.7 Technotone's custom flaming speaker grill.

8.8 Technotone at 2002 Summer CPL.

The Mg3 NeXT Cube

Every underground community has its stars and legends. For modders, one of those stars is Barry Collins, a.k.a Cold Dog. Just to give you an idea of how new true case modding is, even Cold Dog has only been at it since early 2000.

Cold Dog was inspired by another early modder—Ultragooey. Cold Dog started tinkering with his cases after he saw Ultragooey's Unreal Case on the [Hard]OCP forums in 2000. Looking at the case now, few real modders would be impressed. It has a blue paint job, a Plexiglas window, an Unreal Tournament logo, and a few lights thrown inside. But Cold Dog calls it "the granddaddy of all present-day case mods," and adds, "The 'Battle of the Beige' had begun with that case." Cold Dog wasn't the only one to be inspired by Ultragooey's work. He says it "became one of those phenomenal things that happen on the Internet sometimes." But unlike Mahir and a pack of dancing hamsters, case mods seem to be here to stay.

"Case modding draws many parallels to hot-rodding or custom motorcycle building," says Cold Dog. "A little bit of craftsmanship and design to create a product that has flash and power—in a geeky kinda way."

Mods come in two main categories. There are the customized cases created with interesting materials, fancy paint jobs, windows, and lights inside. And then there are the cases made from something entirely different, like Lord Pheaton's computer made out of an old console radio or KiSA's case made out of an old bomb tail assembly. Cold Dog's most noted work is a bit of both. It's an old PC case with a custom PC inside. But this isn't just any old case. In fact, the computer it was built for wasn't even technically a PC. It's a NeXT cube—the perfect 12-inch cubed computers that were built to run the NeXTStep operating system, the brainchild of Steve Jobs in his years away from Apple. NeXT produced only 50,000 of these cubes, which were made out of magnesium and painted black. During their years in existence (1988–1993), they sold for a whopping $9,995. In December of 2001, Cold Dog found a NeXT case seller online, and the rest is modding history. He calls his case the Mg3, or magnesium cubed.

For this project, Cold Dog used the following supplies:

- NeXT case
- Aluminum mounting plates for the motherboard and drives
- Vacuum Fluorescent Display (VFD)
- Homemade fan control
- Cold cathode fluorescent lamp (CCFL) lighting
- Plexiglas

Current hardware includes the following:

- Intel D850MD motherboard
- 512MB Rambus
- P4/2.2 CPU
- PNY GF4 Ti 4600 video card

When Cold Dog announced on the Pheaton forums
(`www.pheatonforums.com/phpBB2/viewtopic.php?t=137`) that he'd be working
with magnesium, the folks on the boards warned him about the dangerous properties
of the metal. But he wasn't worried. Cold Dog is currently a research technician for a
chemical company, but for many years, he worked as a pipe fitter where he fabricated
pipe and sheet steel. He's been grinding and welding all kinds of metals for the past 30
years.

Barry's first step was to remove the paint from the case. That's when he made an interesting discovery. "I kinda stumbled across the fact that when it was scratched, the magnesium was real shiny," he says. "So, I set about to strip off all the paint and polish it up
with sandpaper and rubbing compounds." He then spent several weeks working the
cube over with different grits of sandpaper and different brands of rubbing compounds. In total, he estimates that it took him 33 hours of sanding and polishing
by hand.

"The result was pretty impressive if I say so myself," says Cold Dog.

But he's not the only one who was impressed. When he first revealed his cube on the
Pheaton forums, the gasps of awe in subsequent posts were almost audible. The stunning cube shone like polished chrome. See Figures 8.9 and 8.10. Because Barry had
posted his work as he went along, the folks on the forums knew just how much dedi-
cation he'd put into this project.

Although the polished magnesium looked like chrome, it wasn't. And as a result, it suf-
fered from tarnishing, smudging, and oxidation. Cold Dog found that the cube would
lose its shine easily and even fingerprints would leave permanent marks. After experi-
menting with different car waxes, he finally decided on carnauba wax. It allowed the
cube to keep its shine for weeks.

8.9 The polished NeXT cube.

8.10 Rear view of the NeXT cube.

Some modders plan everything in advance. Not Cold Dog. "I'm terrible at planning," he says. "I get an idea and tend to run with it. Development happens during the actual building." Still, he advises, it helps to work from the outside in. "The primary thing of importance is the enclosure," he says. "Once the enclosure is built, the bells and whistles can be added later."

Cold Dog's bells and whistles included chrome fans with homemade controls, aluminum mounting plates for the mobo and drives, a VFD, CCFL lighting, and a little Plexiglas. He also kept the logo and original serial number. And for true authenticity, he picked up an actual NeXT power cord on eBay. Of course, not everything on the original case stayed. He did away with outdated parts like the fan grill, which he says only allows for 50 percent ventilation.

Many mods get taken on field trips to LAN parties, (gatherings of gamers playing against one another on one local area network) but most of them usually just end up gracing the computer rooms of the modders who created them. However, some lucky custom cases get to leave home and head out to see the world. While Cold Dog was creating the NeXT cube, Intel asked him to build a custom gaming PC for its gaming booth at the tech conventions. He suggested the NeXT cube, and the company jumped at the idea. When the cube left his house in May 2002, it had an Intel D850MD motherboard, 512MB Rambus, a P4/2.2 CPU, and a PNY GF4 Ti4600 video card, which were all top-of-the-line components at the time.

Since then, the NeXT case has been all over the world with Intel Europe. Recently, Intel contacted Cold Dog to ask if it could send the case back to him to get a polish and some hardware upgrades.

The Humidor Series

Sometimes a cigar case is not just a cigar case.

The idea for the Humidor series began more than 10 years ago. That's when Jeffrey L. Stephenson first started thinking about building a PC case out of wood. "I'd been lurking in the online modding community for the last several years watching innovations and trends," he says. Jeffrey thought a wood PC tower would be too expensive and take too much time, until he came up with the idea for the HumidorPC. See Figures 8.11 and 8.12.

8.11 HumidorPC.

8.12 Rear view of the HumidorPC.

"I wanted to build a computer that was unusual and distinct yet still have a marketable angle," says Jeffrey. Enter the humidor.

For the Humidor series project, Jeffrey used the following supplies:

- Humidors
- Lights
- Cooling fans
- Grills
- Cable sleeving
- ATX harnesses
- 12-volt DC motors (3)
- 2 feet of 1/4-inch cable mesh
- 1 1/2 feet of 1/2-inch cable mesh
- 40mm finger guard (chrome)
- 60mm finger guard (chrome)
- Dollhouse wood door frame (for molding on one of the openings)
- Decals for glass top
- 633 model Crystalfontz control panel module (for the Humidor V)

Hardware (for the Humidor M) included the following:

- VIA EPIA M 933 MHz
- 512MB PC2100 RAM
- 15GB hard drive
- Windows XP Home SP1
- 16X slimline DVD
- ATI Remote Wonder
- Microsoft 802.11b USB client
- Microsoft Bluetooth keyboard and mouse
- Crystalfontz USB LCD display

- ThermalTake Tiger 1 HSF anodized in red (used to replace the stock CPU cooler)
- ThermalTake Active Memory Cooler anodized in red
- 4-port powered USB2.0 hub
- Vantec Stealth 60mm exhaust fan

"The fact is that cigar humidors have been on the desks of successful executives for decades," he says. "In the movies we saw associates being invited into the office and offered a cigar from the humidor. On *Hogan's Heroes*, they were always stealing cigars from Colonel Klink's humidor."

In July 2002, Jeffrey built the first in the Humidor series—the Humidor64. It was a crude machine that he used mainly for thermal testing. Modders who choose unlikely materials always need to be conscious of heat issues, and Jeffrey is no different. Not only was he putting a PC inside a wooden box, he also intended to keep the box closed for aesthetic reasons. In September of that same year, Jeffrey improved on the design with the Humidor II. This time he used a glass top. See Figure 8.13.

8.13 Humidor with glass top.

"I mounted wireless transceivers inside the box for keyboard, mouse, and Internet access," says Jeffrey. "My goal was to reduce the number of cables outside the humidor to make it look more appealing."

The series grew from there. Soon the motherboard manufacturer, VIA, got wind of Jeffrey's creations and sent him the VIA EPIA-M and EPIA-V boards to work with. Thus, the Humidor M and the Humidor V were born. See Figure 8.14.

8.14 Humidor V.

Jeffrey says he didn't start keeping track of costs until he started the Humidor V project. As an exercise in mass production and economies of scale, Jeffrey built 10 identical Humidor V computers, carefully documenting the construction process and tracking all his costs. That's when he found out he could get some great deals by buying in bulk. He used an 800 MHz board and a Vantec 60mm Stealth cooling fan to control heat issues.

Now Jeffrey sells the Humidor V to executives who want a classy looking desk accessory that's also a computer. The Humidor V comes in oak, rosewood, and cherry. "It looks good. It's very quiet. It can color coordinate with the rest of the office, and it is very exclusive, so far," Jeffrey adds, hopefully.

Jeffrey has also designed HumidorPCs for the home. The Humidor M runs the VIA EPIA-M, which was designed for multimedia applications. This gave Jeffrey the idea to turn the machine into a living room entertainment device. He installed an ATI Remote Wonder transceiver, a Microsoft Bluetooth keyboard and mouse, a Microsoft 802.11b USB transceiver, a DVD drive, built-in 5.1 audio, and TV-out. The folks at VIA were so impressed they flew Jeffrey from Florida to Vegas to show off his work at the Consumer Electronics Show (CES).

"The HumidorPC series is an exercise in 'new thinking,'" says Jeffrey. "Computers don't have to be ugly or all the same." Even though the HumidorPCs are no longer technically "one of a kind" pieces, they're still a far cry from those boring old beige boxes. Because humidors come in all shapes and sizes, Jeffrey is constantly coming up with unique new mods. Right now he's working on an art deco humidor with a P4 processor.

Jeffrey's creativity doesn't stop with the humidor either. He says he once installed a computer inside an ATX power supply. He mounted the power supply inside an empty case, hooked it up, and started the "empty" computer.

"As far as I know," says Jeffrey, "case modding is the only creative outlet for pure hardware geeks."

AMD Big Block

Newbies who accidentally stumble upon the modding community on the web might wonder what the point is to all this case decoration if your computer is just going to sit tucked away under your desk. Although some case mods are the showpieces of their owners' living rooms, one of the reasons people started customizing cases was to have something to show off at LAN parties. To really intimidate your fellow gamers, the last thing you want to do is show up with a standard beige box.

Rainer Wingende, a.k.a heaDrOOMx, says he's been customizing his cases long before people started calling it "modding." He created his award-winning AMD Big Block not just to show off but out of necessity. "At LAN parties," he says, "I always needed two PCs—one for gaming and one for an FTP server." That's how he came up with the idea for the AMD Big Block's V8 engine. A V8 engine for a car consists of two rows of four cylinders connected in a V shape. Instead of the two rows of cylinders, Rainer used two mini PC towers. See Figure 8.15.

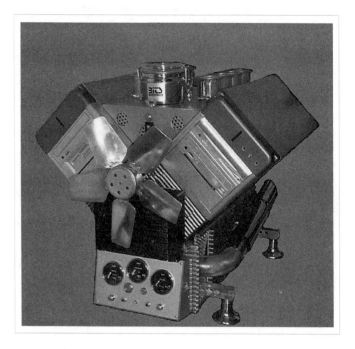

8.15 AMD Big Block.

For this project, Rainer used the following supplies:

Left side:

- Mini tower with PSU (28 ultrabright red LEDs inside)
- MSI KT4 ULTRA-BSR
- AMD XP-Thoroughbred 2200
- 512MB DDR-RAM PC333
- CL2,5, Samsung
- GeForce4 (ASUS V8420) with 128MB
- NIC
- TV card
- 20GB Maxtor
- 60GB Western Digital
- 30GB Seagate
- DVD/CDRW
- LS120
- Enermax 435 (no PFC)
- LED meter behind the small smoke glass stripe in the left front bezel

Right side:

- Chopped mini tower, mounted on the left side at a 90-degree angle
- HEC-PSU
- Shuttle Spacewalker HOT591P (Baby-AT with ATX-features), turned 180 degrees
- AMD K6-2/450 (without heat spreader)
- 256MB SD-RAM PC133
- RIVA TNT 16MB
- CMD UDMA100 IDE Controller
- NIC
- ESS sound card with built-in amplifier (SPK-out/Line-out/Line-in/MIC)
- 40GB Maxtor

- Phillips 8fach-CDRW
- No-name 44× CD-ROM
- HEC 300W (no PFC) PSU
- 28 ultrabright red LEDs inside
- A second LED meter behind the small smoke glass stripe in the right front bezel
- CPU with built-in air tunnel system for more efficient passive cooling
- 5-port network switch (10/100)

Top:

- Eight fake air intakes with red LEDs inside
- Cheap stainless steel reservoir with self-welded nozzles

Bottom:

- Water pump
- Digital voice recorder
- IC amplifier
- Speakers
- Copper radiator powered with a 120mm Papst fan
- Flywheel from an old 1959 DKW-Munga, powered by a small gearbox
- Old cooling plates
- Left and right side exhausts made from two silencers of a chopper
- Converter 12/24 volts
- Ceramic resistors for tuning the Smith gauges
- Cable
- Wires
- Tubes

The front panel:

- Three original Smith gauges from a 1969 Lotus Europa
- Knobs for the fan start buttons, sound, and key lock

One of the mini towers contains the motherboard, cards, and the PSU. The other half of the V holds a second motherboard that Rainer calls his "accelerator engine." He uses the accelerator engine for data storage and backup, "so that I can game with the main engine and transfer data with the accelerator engine at the same time at a LAN party."

The V8 engine was inspiration for function as well as form. Rainer calls the Big Block a tribute to the V8 engine. When he was 18 years old, he and a friend owned a 1971 Ford Mustang with a BOSS engine, which he loved because it had more power than he would ever need. That's the same way he feels about the AMD Big Block.

Rainer continued the automotive theme throughout the PC case. On the base of the Big Block he included a small digital voice recorder, an IC amplifier, and speakers that play the startup sounds of a V8 engine. He also added silencers from an old motorcycle as the exhausts and a copper radiator with a flywheel from a 1959 DKW-Munga (the old German army jeep). The front panel even contains original Smith gauges from Rainer's old 1969 Lotus. But the gauges aren't just for show. The left and the middle gauges display the 12 volts of the PSU, and the right one shows the temperature of the passive-cooled CPU.

Although Rainer used many recycled parts for the Big Block, he says the project cost him about $3000. It also took 250 hours of work, more than 10 gallons of caffeine, lots of beer (if something didn't work), and Italian wine (if it did). For more about the Big Block, check out **www.headroomx.com**.

If he had an unlimited budget, Rainer says his next project would be to create a mod, "which is built in a robot, able to walk on its own two feet, and controlled by a separate PC." He adds that the mod would be able to set itself up at a LAN party and lay down the keyboard, mouse, and monitor. It would only need someone to plug in the power cord.

Like many other modders, Rainer says that when he's planning a project, his friends and neighbors always doubt that his ideas will ever work. "At first some neighbors said I was silly," Rainer says. But now that his award-winning cases have appeared several times on television and in newspapers in his native Germany, they think he's a genius. But he knows he's really just the same modder he's always been and always will be.

The ToAsTOr

If you cut a window into your PC case, you're a modder. If you build a PC inside a 1960 General Electric toaster, you're a modern artist.

In his former life as a network admin, Joe Klingler often needed extra cooling for his hard drives, so he began to build cases with windows and custom mounted fans. These were his first mods, and they made him long for something more unique. So, he got the germ of an idea and started to scour the antique stores.

Joe had some practical concerns as he searched for the perfect piece. "I wanted something built out of metal for RFI and EMI shielding," says Joe. He also wanted something small enough to be portable.

Finally, he found the chrome 1960 GE toaster with a "sizeable crumb tray." The antique was just large enough to fit the guts of a PC, but still small enough to fit into a bag to take to a friend's house or to work. Joe says he didn't buy it right away. Instead, he left to purchase an EPIA motherboard with the Mini-ITX form factor. The maximum mainboard size of the Mini-ITX is only 170mm x 170mm. He then brought the motherboard back to the antique store to see if it would fit inside the toaster. It did. Two weeks and one Dremel later, the ToAsTOr was born.

For this project, Joe used the following supplies:

- 1960 General Electric antique chrome toaster
- LCD screen
- Blue LEDs
- Push and toggle switches
- DC to DC circuit board
- AC to DC external converter
- Steel mailbox mounting straps
- Stainless steel bolts
- Stainless steel washers
- Stainless steel locking nuts with nylon inserts
- Rubber washers
- Fans

- Blue cold cathode and inverter
- Auto trim blackout tape
- Clear auto door trim
- Self-adhesive door insulation foam
- Several square feet of Dynamat
- Nylon ties
- Motherboard standoffs
- Computer screws
- Lots of scrap metal to make brackets

Hardware included the following:

- DVD/CDRW
- 120GB hard drive with 8MB cache
- 800 MHz processor
- 512MB Corsair RAM
- 64MB DDR for video
- Dual head video output with DVI, TV-out
- SPDIF (Digital) audio output

To ready the case, Joe first took it apart and sanded the inside. Then he applied two light coats of Rust-Oleum rusty metal primer. He asserts he once used this primer on an exhaust manifold and had no problems with it, even after years of use. Next he used a motherboard tray from a standard PC and modified it to fit the EPIA mobo. He used steel mailbox mounting strips, stainless steel bolts, SS washers, and SS locking nuts with nylon inserts to keep all the parts in place. See Figure 8.16.

"It took every free moment I was not at work or asleep for two weeks," Joe recalls. "I had to assemble and disassemble it countless times to measure all of the cuts and check for clearances." His Dremel lasted nearly to the end of the project and then it died a quiet death. He tried using a hacksaw to trim the toaster, but that was a disaster. He finally had to borrow a Dremel from a friend to finish the mod.

8.16 Inside the bottom of the ToAsTOr.

In its former life, this toaster was quite a beast to be reckoned with. Back in 1960 it used 1200 watts of power. Now it has a DVD/CDRW drive, 120GB hard drive, and an 800 MHz processor. See Figure 8.17. It dual boots Windows XP Pro and Slackware Linux. Even the toast slot is multifunctional. The custom mounted fans blow air out the hole and CDs and DVDs pop out through the slots like toasted wheat bread. The blue cold cathode gives the ToAsTOr a cool glow, as shown in Figure 8.18.

8.17 Inside the top of the ToAsTOr.

8.18 The ToAsTOr's blue cold cathode.

"I had absolutely no idea how challenging it would be to build," declares Joe. "I thought it would take a few days." But it was all worth it. He uses the ToAsTOr mainly as an MP3 server, DVD player, and for occasional surfing and gaming. See Figure 8.19. Joe calls it his "bedroom system" because it currently lives in his bedroom, where he says "it is so quiet, you can easily fall asleep with it running."

More information about the ToAsTOr can be found at `www.mini-itx.com/projects/toasterpc`.

8.19 Completed ToAsTOr.

Biohazard

The summer of 2000 saw unprecedented layoffs of talented people during the dot-com industry bust. Paul Capello was one of those people. But instead of moping around spending his severance pay on booze and video games, Paul decided to put his creativity to work offline by creating modified computer cases. After some experimentation in the summer of 2001, he started his tribute to H.R. Giger and the *Alien* movies. It became the Alien Case Mod, which was fawned over across the web and then appeared in *Wired* magazine in October 2003. These days Paul is a full-time modder with several award-winning projects under his belt and a successful business creating custom cases.

Paul was honing his artistic talents long before he became a case modder. He grew up fascinated by movie special effects and worked as a carpenter and a prop builder for 15 years. He's also done special makeup effects, mechanical effects, digital effects, and miniature model making for feature films. It was all of these jobs that helped inspire one of Paul's most famous cases: Biohazard: Toxic Case Mod. See Figure 8.20. He calls it "a living comic book and a tribute to all the B-movie monsters born of toxic waste." He adds, "Think *Toxic Avenger* meets *Return of the Living Dead.*"

8.20 Biohazard: Toxic Case Mod.

Paul, a.k.a Crimson Sky, began building Biohazard in late spring of 2003. "I had seen the biohazard stickers, window etchings, and fan grills available and wanted to take the concept a few steps further," he recounts.

For this project, Paul used the following supplies:

- Generic color case
- Life-size human skull kit
- Plastic clock face
- Auto body filler
- Green LED Antec case fan with biohazard grill
- Dual green cathode tubes
- Safety recessed Power and Reset buttons
- Indicator lights
- Front bay door
- Nexus fan controller
- Nexus CPU fan controller
- Clay
- Polymer resin
- Clear epoxy
- Fluorescent green paint

With Biohazard, Paul managed to take everything about modding one step further. One of the amazing things about Paul's work is that he was able to use generic parts to create such a unique PC. He started with a standard color case, and with various parts from model kits, 99-cent stores, and auto parts stores, he fashioned a mod that's worthy of a blockbuster sci-fi flick. In fact, Biohazard is so artistic that when Paul posted pictures of it on a popular case modding forum, some members couldn't believe that the pictures weren't Photoshop fakes. See Figure 8.21.

There is one thing on Biohazard that is fake and thankfully that's the skull on the window. It's made from a life-size human skull kit and a plastic clock face from a thrift store. To make the corroded texture, Paul used auto body filler, which he airbrushed "to make it look rusted and crusty." He molded other parts with polystyrene plastic, which he points out is both strong and flexible. He buys it in sheets, which he cuts into patterns to make the shapes.

8.21 Close-up of the Biohazard mod.

Biohazard's other bells and whistles include dual green cathode tubes that light up the components inside and "The Bio Containment Unit," which contains multiple strobe warnings and indicator lights. In addition, he used clear epoxy mixed with fluorescent green paint to create a slimy, wet look. After he finished the molded parts of the mod, he buffed them with a buffing wheel and sealed them with liquid Turtle Wax. See Figure 8.22.

In total, the case cost about $75. It took Paul about 40 hours to complete the job, during which, he emphasizes, "I consumed more caffeine than given to lab rats when stress testing their nervous systems."

Paul's advice for the newbie modder? "Experience, safety, and respect for the tools is a must."

For more information about the Biohazard, check out
www.thebestcasescenario.com.

8.22 A slimy, wet look; waxed and buffed.

Hemophilia

Like any true art form, inspiration for a mod usually comes from within. For some, it comes from a modder's own blood. That's certainly true for Jerami Campbell and his Hemophilia case.

Jerami has hemophilia, a rare blood disorder that slows the clotting process. "On one of the final days of construction on this case, I cut myself pretty bad," relates Jerami. Because of the look of the case, he was already thinking of naming it after blood, but he reveals "seeing my blood dripping onto the floor made me think of hemophilia, and it just seemed like the perfect name." See Figure 8.23.

8.23 Hemophilia.

For this project, Jerami used the following supplies:

- Red glass
- Aluminum pieces
- Motherboard tray from an old case
- Lian Li bay covers
- Four red cathodes
- Two red LED fans
- 4-port network switch in the back of the case

Hardware included the following:

- Asus A7S333 motherboard
- AMD XP 2200+
- 768MB of PC2100 DDRAM
- Sound Blaster Live!
- D-Link NIC
- Maxtor 40GB 7200 RPM HD
- Lite-On 48× burner
- GigaFast 5-port network switch

Hemophilia, the mod, is a stained glass case made from 146 individually hand cut pieces of red rippled glass and 10 pieces of brushed aluminum cut from a door kickplate. It includes four red cathodes, two red LED fans, and a 4-port network switch on the back of the case. See Figures 8.24 and 8.25. Jerami also used a motherboard tray from an old case and two Lian Li bay covers, popular among the modding community. One of his favorite parts of the case is the way the door slides back through a channel. This was his first attempt at a mechanism like this and he states proudly, "As it turns out, it's the best door I've made so far."

8.24 Side view of Hemophilia.

8.25 Front view of Hemophilia.

Hemophilia took Jerami 62 hours and 19 minutes over the course of three weeks to complete. He experienced many cuts and two serious burns. Not counting the computer components, it cost nearly $400.

Jerami says the inspiration for his project was love. For the computer or for his wife, he does not say. We do, however, get an idea of how his wife feels about his modding obsession from what Jerami calls his fantasy mod. "It is four systems mounted in a giant Plexiglas pyramid on a 5 foot by 5 foot table," declares Jerami. He calls it "The Gaming Pyramid of Death," he says, "because if I built it, my wife would kill me."

Hemophilia isn't Jerami's first mod. He's been creating custom cases since he saw Ed Downing's Olde Yankee Fragger in the November 2001 issue of *Maximum PC* magazine.

"It was the first case that I had seen that was built from scratch, and the craftsmanship was amazing," recalls Jerami. "I wanted to build my own after seeing that case." Jerami has been creating ever since.

With each new case, Jerami seems to build on past ideas to create something more unique. His Stained Glass Computer (`www.lucentrigs.com/Stained%20page01.htm`) served as a testing ground for many of the features he perfected in Hemophilia. The idea for the framed American flag in his award-winning mod called Vehement (`www.lucentrigs.com/Vehement-2.htm`) came from his Framed Computer (`www.lucentrigs.com/Framed%20page01.htm`), which contains the guts of a PC within a deep glass frame.

Hemophilia isn't Jerami's main system. Currently, he uses his newest case, Narcosis. Like Hemophilia, Narcosis sports glass sides, but it also has a homemade lava lamp built out of a glass vase in the front. Because the bulbs used on lava lamps give off a lot of heat, Jerami added two LED fans and created a timer switch that would turn off the bulbs as soon as they created enough heat to get the lava flowing. Right now, Jerami admits, he has two more cases currently under construction; one is made from a three-foot tall Tiki head.

For modders attempting a stained-glass PC project, Jerami offers a few tips. First, he says "use brass channel instead of copper tape on parts that will be used heavily—around the door, on the motherboard tray, and so on." He also warns that you should clean all the fingerprints off the glass before soldering it into place. Once the glass is soldered, you may not be able to reach in to clean it sufficiently. "Don't be scared to handle the components," he adds. "Fear is what keeps you from doing really cool stuff."

The Mailbox Mod

Jeff Neima gives new meaning to the phrase, "going postal." When he was building the Mailbox Mod, friends would come over to his apartment and see computer parts and a destroyed aluminum mailbox strewn across his floor. The first thing they would ask was "Are you okay?" When he told them he was building a PC inside a mailbox, the second thing they asked was, "Are you okay?"

"It's hard for nonmodders to understand," says Jeff.

Jeff started modding after coming across the Virtual-Hideout web site during a late-night surfing session. He acknowledges that he's always been the type of person to take things apart to see how they worked, even if there was a chance they would never work again. "Cutting, drilling, painting, tools, chance of bodily harm—all of these things sparked my creative match," states Jeff. "It was then that I bought my first Dremel."

When Jeff saw what other modders had done to their cases, he knew what he had to do to his. He spray-painted his tower without sanding it, cut out a huge Unreal Tournament logo in the side, and installed a neon light, which he calls a "classic new guy move." Now he says it's "ghastly," but adds, "it was awesome back then."

The Mailbox Mod shows how far Jeff has come. The project took hold when a former employer saw pictures of Jeff's mods and commissioned him to do a customized PC for the company. Because the company specialized in allowing customers to send postal mail directly though an email account, Jeff decided to build a PC inside a mailbox.

"I thought of a classic style, aluminum mailbox," Jeff says. "You know, those kinds of mailboxes you always see on some country road in the middle of nowhere. I started to envision cramming this mailbox with all sorts of hardware, lights, fans, and LEDs. From that point on, I knew I had the perfect idea, and I was hooked on it."

For this project, Jeff used the following supplies:

- Aluminum mailbox
- Sheet metal
- Blue paint (for the sheet metal)
- Rubber molding
- Cathode light
- Blue LEDs

- Switches
- Plexiglas (for the window)
- Epoxy
- 92mm Panaflow fan
- 60mm Panaflow fan
- Shuttle FV-24 motherboard
- Enermax 1U PSU

First on the agenda was finding the right mailbox. After much searching, Jeff located a standard size, thin aluminum mailbox for only $24 at **www.thesolargroup.com**. When it arrived, he found that the Shuttle FV-24 motherboard he'd chosen for the project fit perfectly inside. He was also pleased that the mailbox was light and in good condition with no dents. See Figure 8.26.

8.26 Standard mailbox used for the mod.

The next step was to take apart the mailbox. He removed all the rivets that were used to keep it together and laid out all the pieces. Then he drew an elaborate blueprint for the design. He admits that experience and advanced planning was what helped the mod succeed. "Since this was my fifth computer mod," Jeff says, "I knew the potential pitfalls that might have occurred."

Jeff's next step was to cut windows in the back of the mailbox so he could access the motherboard connectors and the power supply once everything was installed. But because nothing was installed yet, it was tough to figure out where to do the cutting. So Jeff made a cardboard template of the back of the mailbox. He planned the cutouts on the template and transferred it to the back of the mailbox when he was done. Jeff attributes this last stroke of genius to his girlfriend. "Girls who love modding rock," he says.

After mounting the motherboard, CD-ROM, and hard drive, Jeff cut a hole in the front of the box and added a wire mesh grill for proper airflow. Then he used his Dremel to cut a large window in the side of the mailbox so admirers could see his work on the inside, as shown in Figure 8.27.

8.27 Side window of the mailbox.

Next he fashioned all the brackets and mounts by hand out of sheet metal. Finally, he added a fan (which he painted himself), a cathode, some blue LEDs, and a handful of switches from Radio Shack. See Figure 8.28.

"Between a full-time job as a software engineer, a full-time girlfriend, and surfing for an hour every morning, there was not much time to work on the mailbox mod," says Jeff. (By the way, he means surfing off the beaches of San Diego, not the forums of HardOCP, although he does that, too.) "However," he adds, "I did find about an hour every night and some hours on the weekend to go into modding mode." Working in the middle of the night was how he found out how loud the meeting of a Dremel and a piece of aluminum could be, even when he was working in the closet to avoid waking his neighbors.

8.28 Inside components of the mailbox.

In total, the project took six weeks to complete. See Figure 8.29. During that time, Jeff sustained a few injuries, the worst being several slices by sharp pieces of sheet metal. "This could have been solved by wearing a pair of leather gloves," admits Jeff, "but you just don't get the same hands-on feeling when doing that."

For more details about Jeff's mod, check out `www.neima.com/mailboxmod01.shtml`.

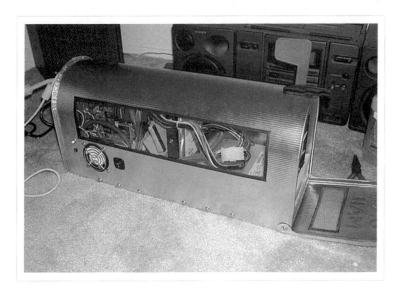

8.29 The completed mailbox mod.

Wood Case

Mikko Syrjälä isn't the first person to build a PC case out of wood, but his may very well be the most attractive. He built every detail of the case by hand—right down to the four-paned glass window on the side of the case that looks like it belongs on a rustic log cabin.

Mikko explains that he's been building and modifying machines long before the term "case modder" became popular. He can't even remember his first mod, but he says it was probably before personal computers existed and was something "not so useful." He started the wood case mod in autumn 2002 after deciding that his current case was too small. At that point, all he knew was that he wanted to build a case mod that was more than just paint, windows, and lights. So he made a few measurements and began building.

For this project, Mikko used the following supplies:

- Wood
- Wheels
- Lights
- LCD
- LEDs
- Copper-plate
- Window glass
- Hinges
- Keylock
- Peltier cooler
- Pewter
- Hot glue
- Wiring
- Relay
- Connectors
- Fans
- Switches
- AMD sticker
- Screws
- Old AT power unit

Mikko admits that he had no major plans or blueprints for the case. He didn't even make a single sketch of how he intended it to look. As a result, the entire project took more than three months of his free time. In fact, it took him four tries just to get the front panel of the case right. But he didn't mind. Because this is only his hobby, Mikko acknowledges that he likes to work slowly to savor the project and to avoid injury.

Much of the wood case is made from recycled parts from other machines. In fact, Mikko says 90 percent of the case comes from salvaged parts. These pieces include an old car radiator, Eheim pumps from a fish tank, and furniture feet. He also cut pieces from his old Englight case to mount the motherboard and CD-ROM drive. "If it's good and not broken," says Mikko, "why throw it away, if you can use it?"

Mikko takes the comparison of hot-rodders and case modders to a new level. He found an old ignition lock at a junk store and installed it in the front of the PC. To turn on the PC, just turn the key. See Figure 8.30.

8.30 Ignition lock on the wood case.

Other miscellaneous tools and parts include copper-plate, window glass, hinges, pewter, hot glue, wiring, relay, fans, switches, and an old AT power unit. But Mikko contends that the most important elements in this project were imagination, and of course, lots of wood.

The authentic window on the side of the case is clever and attractive, as shown in Figure 8.31, but the front of the case is even more interesting.

The CD-ROM tray pops out from behind a clean wood face, below which Mikko built a round cabinet door (see Figure 8.32).

8.31 Side view of the wood case.

8.32 CD-ROM case and round cabinet door.

Inside the cabinet is a mini-bar with perfect compartments for CDs, bottles, and even drinks that are ingeniously kept cold by the PC's Peltier watercooling system (see Figure 8.33).

You can see the cooling at work through a small window Mikko placed above the cabinet, lit by green LEDs. See Figure 8.31.

In addition, the front of the case sports a small LCD for system stats. Mikko admits that his LCD wasn't the best, so he placed it in at an angle and backlit it with two more LEDs so that the readout can now be seen from some distance.

8.33 Inside the cabinet.

Mikko says he has no background or training in woodworking, he just enjoys it. His advice for modders (or anyone else) is to do whatever you want today because tomorrow it may be too late.

For more information about Mikko's mod, check out `http://koti.mbnet.fi/jmsthrd`.

The Tech Tube

Anyone who's spent any time in the modding community knows of Troy "T-Bone" Ervin, creator of the MicroSoft Oven (a PC in a microwave) and innovator of the Water Tower (a case window filled with bubbling water). One of T-Bone's lesser-known creations is the Tech Tube, a futuristic looking case that he created from one of those combination trash can ashtrays you often see outside hotels. See Figure 8.34.

8.34 Tech Tube.

"I saw it in the dumpster," says T-Bone, "and it was the right size, and it looked like all the parts would fit, or I could make all the parts fit."

An engineer by trade, T-Bone spends a lot of time working in AutoCAD. He used the program to design the Tech Tube mod in 2001. "It sat in my mod folder for about a year," he admits. "As motherboards got smaller and faster, it was time to bring the mod to life."

For this project, T-Bone used the following components:

- Combination trash can/ashtray
- Plexiglas
- Motherboard
- CPU
- Memory
- PSU
- Neon lights

The first thing T-Bone did was cut off the top and bottom of the trash can ashtray and sand it down until it was nice and smooth. The PC is actually split into two pieces, the bottom part of the case holds the PSU, hard drive, and CD-ROM. It also includes a fan to push the hot air out. The top part of the case, which holds the motherboard and the CPU, contains another fan to push the hot air out. After T-Bone had controlled the airflow, it was time for the bells and whistles. The Tech Tube is illuminated from the inside with neon lights and has a hologram reflector, hand-curved Plexiglas cover. See Figure 8.35.

8.35 Inside the Tech Tube; seen through the curved Plexiglas cover.

In total T-Bone says it took him about four weeks and $500 to build the Tech Tube. It turned out just as he imagined it. "Maybe even better," he adds.

The case was originally called the TimeBomb, but T-Bone explains that Intel asked him to change the name out of respect for those that lost their lives on September 11th. T-Bone sold the case to Intel, and the company now uses it regularly to show off its hardware at trade shows. Intel liked his work so much that these days it sends him all the latest Intel products for his modding creations. In fact, T-Bone was the first to be chosen to be part of Intel's elite corps of modders, which now includes several others in this book.

In addition to the Tech Tube, T-Bone has an admirable collection of mods including the aforementioned MicroSoft Oven, the Water Tower, and the ultra-cool "Portable" PC, which is made out of an aluminum briefcase. If money and time were not an issue, T-Bone reveals, he'd create a LAN-party rig out of a Hummer2. "Now that's what you call real mobile computing," he says.

The LokiCube

Most modders take a while to perfect their art. Not Tino Stephan. The LokiCube was only his second mod project, but it was so good that it won him third place in the German "Modder of the Year" contest.

The LokiCube is a water-cooled cubic computer made almost entirely from 3mm anodized aluminum. Even the Reset and Power switches are aluminum. The 14.5-inch tall cube rests on four wooden blocks, presumably to help with airflow. Tino had the laser etchings on the case professionally done (see Figure 8.36), but the rest of the cube is purely his handmade creation. The LokiCube has a simple and elegant design, but it's also functional. Tino says a cube is the most efficient way he's found to fit PC components into the smallest space possible.

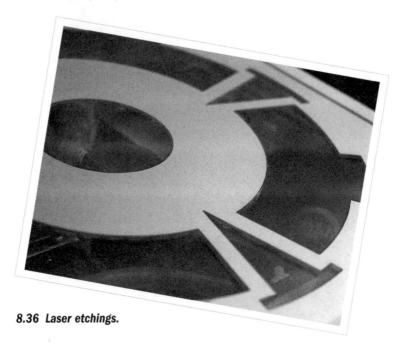

8.36 Laser etchings.

The front of the LokiCube is basically flat. There's a tiny hatch that opens to reveal the CD/DVD player as well as additional LCDs that show the water temperature, exhaust air, and fan voltage. See Figures 8.37 and 8.38.

8.37 The aluminum LokiCube.

8.38 Bottom area of the LokiCube.

The case also features a Plexiglas window through which you can easily see the handful of multicolored LEDs inside. See Figure 8.39.

The cube shape offers some unique challenges. Tino designed a special mount for the motherboard so he wouldn't have to take apart the entire cube every time he wanted to change a single component. The case also has to be specially ventilated because the parts are in such a small space.

Perhaps the success of the LokiCube is due to Tino's planning and preparation. Before he started the project, he designed everything with AutoCAD. He says he built the case in about six months, but he's still changing small things here and there.

Currently, Tino studies computer science in Germany. He organizes regular LAN parties with friends who call him Loki (hence the mod's name). You can find out more about him and his upcoming projects at `www.loki.onlinehome.de`.

8.39 Plexiglas window.

Index

H-I

J-K

L

M

Q-R

S